MANDARIN

BLUE

RAF Chinese Linguists in the Cold War, 1951 – 1962

Reginald Hunt
Geoffrey Russell
Keith Scott

HURUSCO BOOKS

OXFORD 2008

© Reginald Hunt, Geoffrey Russell, Keith Scott 2008
Mandarin Blue

ISBN 978-0-9560235-0-6

Published by Hurusco Books
84 Butler Close
Oxford
OX2 6JQ
email: RAFChinese@gmail.com

Front cover:
The Peak on Hong Kong Island – 1860 by Artist Unknown
Design by Matthew Hunt

Book designed by Michael Walsh at
THE BETTER BOOK COMPANY

A division of
RPM Print & Design
2-3 Spur Road
Chichester
West Sussex
PO19 8PR

DEDICATION

This book is dedicated to the group of young RAF National Servicemen, and the small number of regular airmen, who trained as Chinese Linguists and then carried out radio intercept duties in Hong Kong, during the early Cold War years of 1951-1962.

The authors would also like to acknowledge the RAF administrators, language teachers and attached Chinese civilian instructors, and the lecturers of the School of Oriental & African Studies, London University, who made all this possible.

ROYAL AIR FORCE
WYTHALL

CONTENTS

PREFACE

This book has truly been a collaborative effort between the authors named on the title page. All three have read through and commented on all parts of the book, but for practical reasons each chapter was assigned to one or other of them for drafting and final shaping. So with that proviso, chapters 3, 6, 7 and 13 are the work of Reginald Hunt, chapters 5, 8, 9, 10 and 12 that of Geoffrey Russell and chapters 2, 4 and 14 that of Keith Scott, with chapter 1 being jointly written by Messrs. Russell and Scott and chapter 11 by Messrs. Hunt and Russell. Keith Scott was primarily responsible for preparing the Timeline, Table of Courses and Bibliography.

Sadly, at this late stage, mention must be made of the untimely death of Geoffrey Russell just when the book had been completed and was being prepared for publication. As is evident from the previous paragraph, Geoffrey produced more of the text of the book than either of the other two authors, and he was deeply involved in the interviewing and research which have made this study possible. His two fellow authors benefitted greatly from his thoughtful and perceptive critiquing of their efforts, always based on his own solid values and personal integrity; but more than that, he will be missed as a warm-hearted and constant good companion, and as a true friend. Ever since those days of studying Chinese together more than fifty years ago, he had been an integral member of that closely-knit group of RAF National Servicemen to which the three authors belonged. We acknowledge with sincere thanks the financial contribution made on Geoffrey's behalf by his two daughters Miriam and Faith towards the cost of publishing this book. We are also grateful to Terry Keyms who, after Geoffrey's death, stepped in and gave valuable advice and support during the final stages of publication.

No less important than the work of the three authors has been the contribution of those who willingly shared their memories of and reflections on their time in the services half a century and more ago, and generously granted permission to reproduce their words.

i

We are especially grateful to Paddy Raine (more formally Flt Lt the Rev P J W Raine), and to the following course members (listed chronologically by course and alphabetically within courses): Mick Rice (SOAS 1951-52); John Packer (SOAS 1952-53 and 1953-54); an unnamed member of the 1952-53 SOAS course; John Hampson (SOAS 1953-55); David Raderecht and Don Rimmington (SOAS 1955-57); Alan Barr, Alan Davis, Max Dolby, Steve Fletcher, Peter Gardiner, Terry Keyms, Bernard Morton and other members of No. 1 Course; Mike Grindley, John Norrish and Peter Treacher (No. 3 Course); Bill Mellows (No. 4 Course); James McMullen, Peter Shortell and Donald Sutton (No. 5 Course); Philip Cline, Lawrie Cooke, John Henty and Mike Prada (No. 6 Course); David Iliff and Mike Wallace (No. 7 Course); Ken Brooks (No. 8 Course); Mike Greenall (No. 9 Course); Keith Drury, Ken May and Kenneth Wilson (No. 11 Course). In addition to ransacking their memories Mike Grindley, John Henty and James McMullen generously gave us access to their extensive collections of memorabilia and diaries from their service days; David Iliff kindly read through several chapters in draft form, and his comments enabled us to correct some important errors of fact which might otherwise have gone undetected; and Kenneth Wilson contributed the valuable note on the history of Batty's Belvedere which has been included as an Appendix.

We appreciate the help and advice that we have received from Peter Goodchild, a former officer-instructor in Russian at Pucklechurch; Dave Haysom, John Partridge and other members of RAFLING (The RAF Linguists' Association); Bernard Meadows, who suggested some of the introductory quotations to the chapters; Dr Harold Shukman, Emeritus Fellow of St. Antony's College, Oxford and co-author of *Secret Classrooms* (see bibliography); and Andrew Suddaby, Historian of the 367 SU Association. We also acknowledge the excellent facilities of the National Archives, Kew, London and the Bodleian Library, Oxford, and the contribution to our physical and mental wellbeing made by the Victory Services Club and Chinatown's New World Restaurant in London, Brown's Restaurant in Oxford and Huffkin's Tea Room in Witney; all of these fine establishments provided comfortable and congenial surroundings for many a productive meeting. Peter Bernasconi, John Henty and Bernard Morton kindly gave us permission to reproduce photographs taken by themselves or other materials in their possession, and Matthew Hunt applied his considerable technical and creative talents to the design of the cover and to readying the illustrations for publication. To all of the above we express our heartfelt thanks and appreciation, and we offer sincere apologies to any whose names may have been inadvertently omitted from the list.

As is customary the authors take full responsibility for all the shortcomings of this book. They are aware that much is still not known about the events which it endeavours to cover, and it should be regarded as a pioneering effort and a foundation on which others will, we hope, seek to build in the future. For their benefit, and on the remote chance that there will be a revised edition of this book, the authors will be pleased to receive any corrections and any new information from others who were involved at the time and whom regrettably they have not so far succeeded in contacting. They may be most conveniently reached through the project's email address, *RAFChinese@gmail.com.*

Since it was not possible to use all of the materials collected in preparation for writing this book, the authors propose to deposit them in an appropriate archive, where subject to certain restrictions to protect the privacy of individuals they will be available for consultation by future investigators into this byway of twentieth century military history.

Last but not least, the point needs to be made that the story which we are telling here is above all a human story, and is in no way intended as an exposé of intelligence matters nor as a commentary on the activities of government bodies. True to the spirit of our generation and the times during which we served, we have avoided including any potentially sensitive information – what little we knew – which might even at this late stage be considered as prejudicial to national security. Where it was necessary or desirable to refer to the work which linguists were trained to perform during the Cold War years, we have largely drawn on earlier publications and on documents that are publicly available in the National Archives. If any information that could be remotely construed as security-sensitive has inadvertently passed through our own screening system, we express our sincere regrets.

The Authors

July 2008

TIMELINE

(Events directly connected with the subject matter of this book are shown in bold type)

1945 (8 May)	German surrender, end of War in Europe
1945 (2 September)	Japanese surrender, end of War in the Pacific
1946 (5 March)	Winston Churchill's 'Iron Curtain' speech at Westminster College, Fulton, Missouri, generally held to mark start of the Cold War
1947 (July)	**National Service Act passed by Parliament; term of service provisionally set at twelve months**
1948 (18 December)	**National Service Amendment Act passed, extending term of service to eighteen months**
1949	**First RAF Russian language school established at Kidbrooke (SE London)**
1949 (1 January)	**Official start of National Service (Act and Amendment Act came into force)**

v

1949 (1 October)	Establishment of the Chinese People's Republic under leadership of Mao Zedong, Zhou Enlai and others; border between mainland and Hong Kong sealed off Guomindang (KMT/Chinese Nationalist) regime withdrew to Taiwan
1950	Estimated population of Hong Kong c. 2 million
1950 (25 June)	Outbreak of the Korean War; British troops sent to join United Nations forces on the Korean peninsula **National Service extended from 18 months to 2 years**
1950 (25 October)	Chinese intervention in the Korean War
1951 (25 May)	Guy Burgess and Donald Maclean, SIS (MI6) agents, defected to the Soviet Union.
1951 (September)	**Joint Services School for Linguists (JSSL) established; Russian courses started in former army camp at Bodmin (Cornwall); each course followed by technical**

training at RAF Wythall (S of Birmingham)

1951-52	**First Russian interpreters' courses started at London School of Slavonic and East European Studies (SSEES) and Cambridge University First Chinese course for RAF linguists started at London School of Oriental and African Studies (SOAS), students housed at RAF Uxbridge**
1952-55	**Chinese courses for RAF linguists continued at SOAS, with a new course starting each year and lasting for nine months, followed by 1 month of technical training at Wythall**
1952 (6 February)	Death of King George VI, succeeded by Elizabeth II
1952 (October)	**First contingent of RAF Chinese linguists arrived in Hong Kong to join No. 367 Signals Unit, billetted at Lyemun camp (near Shaukiwan) but working at**

	Batty's Belvedere (on Victoria Peak)
1953 (spring)	**Quarters for linguists in Hong Kong moved from Lyemun to new permanent camp at Little Sai Wan**
1953 (26 June)	Armistice, end of active phase of Korean War
1954-55	1st Taiwan Straits crisis
1954 (17 June)	Britain established diplomatic relations with the Chinese People's Republic at the chargé d'affaires level
1955	**JSSL Russian language courses moved from Bodmin to Crail (Fifeshire)**
1955 (October)	**First RAF-run Chinese course (designated No. 1 Course) started at Wythall, with this and most subsequent courses lasting a full year (including one month of technical training)**
	Students drawn from No. 1 Course (and later from Nos. 3 and 5 Courses) selected as officer cadets, sent to study at

	SOAS for the balance of their National Service
1956 (April)	**No. 2 Course started at Wythall**
1956 (June)	**No. 2 Course moved from Wythall to Worth Matravers (Dorset)**
1956 (October)	**No. 3 Course started at Worth Matravers, first RAF-trained linguists (from No. 1 Course) arrived in Hong Kong during riots involving pro-Nationalist and pro-communist elements** Anglo-French intervention in Egypt (Suez crisis)
1956 (November)	Anti-Soviet uprising in Hungary
1957 (April)	**No. 2 Course finished technical training at Wythall, No. 3 Course moved from Worth Matravers to Pucklechurch (nr. Bristol); No. 4 Course started at Pucklechurch Government White Paper published foreshadowing end of National Service**

1957 (October)	**No. 5 Course started at Pucklechurch**
1958-63	'Great Leap Forward' in China (2nd Five Year Plan)
1958 (April)	**No. 6 Course started at Pucklechurch**
1958 (July)	**Flying saucers sighted over Little Sai Wan**
1958 (August-October)	2nd Taiwan Straits crisis; Communist forces shelled offshore islands
1958 (October)	**No. 7 Course started at Pucklechurch**
1959	Dispute between China and the Soviet Union became public Extension to Kai Tak airport in Hong Kong opened
1959 (April)	**No. 8 Course started at Pucklechurch**
1959 (September)	**All JSSL courses moved to Tangmere (Sussex)**
1959 (October)	**No. 9 Course started at Tangmere**

1959 (December)	RAF Wythall closed permanently, RAF Pucklechurch 'reduced to inactivity status'
1960 (April)	**No. 10 Course started at Tangmere**
1960 (October)	**Last RAF Chinese course (No. 11) started at Tangmere**
1960 (17 November)	Last National Service intake into armed forces
1960	**JSSL officially closed down, direct responsibility for training Chinese linguists (civilians) passed to GCHQ (Government Communications Headquarters)** Estimated population of Hong Kong c. 3 million
1961	**Civilianisation of operations at Batty's Belvedere under way; some reports of low morale and breaches of security**
1961 (March)	Gordon Lonsdale (Konon Molody), former student of Chinese at SOAS, convicted of spying for the Soviet Union

1961 (13 August)	Construction of the Berlin Wall began, escalation of the Cold War
1962 (October)	Cuban missile crisis, further escalation of the Cold War
1963 (January)	H.A.R. ('Kim') Philby, SIS (MI6) agent, defected to the Soviet Union
1963 (16 May)	Last National Serviceman demobilised
1964 (1 January)	**SIGINT (Signals Intelligence) operations in Hong Kong formally passed from military to GCHQ control**
1964 (September)	**GCHQ Chinese language courses moved from Tangmere to North Luffenham (Rutland)**
mid-1960s	**Batty's Belvedere closed down, Hong Kong monitoring operations moved to Tai Mo Shan (New Territories)**
1966 (April)	Start of the 'Cultural Revolution' in China

1967-68	Hong Kong disturbed by Cultural Revolution activity, some rioting took place
1970 (October)	RAF Tangmere permanently closed
1971	Estimated population of Hong Kong c. 4 million
1972 (February)	Visit of US President Richard Nixon to China, paving the way for the establishment of diplomatic relations seven years later
1972 (13 March)	Diplomatic relations between Britain and the Chinese People's Republic raised to ambassadorial level
1976 (9 September)	Death of Mao Zedong, first Chairman of the Communist Party of China
1977-81	Deng Xiaoping became *de facto* leader of China, initiated economic reforms
1979	The United States established diplomatic relations with the Chinese People's Republic (1 January); the two countries

	agreed to set up joint listening posts in NW China to monitor Soviet signals
1980	Estimated population of Hong Kong c. 5 million
1982	**Little Sai Wan closed down, Chinese radio satellite transmissions monitored at Chung Hum Kok (S side of Hong Kong island), more allegations of security breaches**
1989 (4 June)	Political protests in Beijing's Tiananmen Square violently suppressed by authorities
1989 (9 November)	Dismantling of the Berlin Wall, symbolic end of the Cold War
1995 (January)	**Chung Hom Kok dismantled, all GCHQ Hong Kong operations transferred to Australian DSD (Defence Signals Department) and moved to Geraldton (W Australia)**
1997 (1 July)	With the British cession of sovereignty, Hong Kong became a 'Special

Administrative Region' of the
Chinese People's Republic

1999   Estimated population of Hong
Kong 6.9 million

1

LOOKING INTO THE MIRROR

*'By looking into the mirror one can see one's own likeness,
and by looking towards the past one can understand the
present.'*

(Chinese proverb)

In 2005 a small group of men realised that, quite unbelievably, it was
the 50th anniversary of their call-up for National Service. Before
this, two members of the group had expended considerable time
and ingenuity in tracing other members, and several reunions had
been held in a restaurant in London's Chinatown. In spite of greying
hair and the incipient disabilities of age, those already around the
table on each occasion immediately recognised each person as he
arrived. How was this so easy? Because they had all spent the best
part of two years living, sleeping and working alongside each other,
often in a state of intense concentration. Why Chinatown? Because
of a common experience in their lives. It was this combination of
circumstances which led, first out of pure nostalgia and secondly out
of a need to understand more about why it was that they had been
thrown together in the first place, to the planning of this book.

Between 1951 and 1962 almost three hundred young men were
selected to study Chinese on courses conducted by or on behalf of the
Royal Air Force. Almost all were conscripted National Servicemen
(sadly for them, there were no women on these courses) and their
role was part of Britain's defence efforts during the early years of
the Cold War. Other languages were taught, principally Russian, in
which over five thousand translators/interpreters were trained, and

a number of detailed accounts of those linguists' experiences have already appeared in print. The Mandarin Chinese courses involved less than one tenth of that number of trainees, and their story has gone virtually unrecorded. It is not a dramatic story, but it deserves to be captured whilst it is still possible to draw on the first-hand memories of those student linguists who learnt to listen in to China, and were sent out to what at that time was a distant and exotic world. The background is a little easier to understand, now that many of the official documents relating to the military Chinese language programme have been made accessible to the public.

* * * * * * *

Throughout much of history both the state and the armed forces which it controls have found it necessary to make use of a number of language-related skills. There have always been people who might be described as military linguists, and who were called upon to interpret whenever men and women from opposing forces were taken prisoner, and there was a need to obtain from such prisoners information – 'intelligence' – about the movements, strengths and intentions of the other side. Often too, in the history of warfare as well as in peacetime, linguists have been employed on more dangerous missions – to go as spies into the territory of an enemy or potential enemy, and to report back with intelligence gathered at first hand.

In the nineteenth and early twentieth centuries – the age of Morse, Tesla and Marconi – telecommunications began to develop rapidly, and military commanders no longer needed to depend upon responses from often uncooperative prisoners in order to obtain reliable intelligence about an enemy's movements and intentions. From then on the telegraph and later the radio became the preferred means of communication between and within armies, and between the commanders of those armies and their political masters. It was soon discovered, however, that signals transmitted by such means could be intercepted, usually in conditions of relative safety at listening

2

posts behind the front lines. Thus from World War I onwards linguists and the operators of telecommunication receivers started to work in close association with one another to identify and translate enemy messages sent over the wires or the air waves. Since it was imperative to discover the content of such messages with the least possible delay, personnel were soon being trained to act simultaneously as both telegraph or radio operators and linguists, to provide immediate translations of intercepts.

Once military authorities became aware that their radio transmissions were liable to be intercepted, elaborate codes and cyphers were devised to protect the security of intelligence. This was not in itself a new development in the history of warfare, but it was given a new emphasis and greater urgency with the increasing use of telecommunications. The code breaker now became a crucial figure, equal in importance to the telegraph or radio operator and the linguist in the intelligence network. All three elements in the monitoring of military communications were brought together with spectacular results during World War II, most notably at Bletchley Park in Bedfordshire ('Station X') where, among other successes, the mysteries of the German Enigma machines were unlocked. It has been convincingly argued that the work done at Bletchley Park may have shortened the war in Europe by as much as a full year.[1]

The intensification of the Cold War towards the end of the 1940s made it clear to the British government that there was a continuing need to give high priority to the collection and analysis of intelligence from potential enemy sources,[2] and to ensure that it had at its disposal personnel trained in sufficient numbers to undertake these tasks competently and efficiently. But how were such personnel to be recruited? While it was politically impossible for the veterans of wartime conscription to be retained in the Services, the heavy commitment to occupation duties in Germany and Japan, the continuing security issues in what still remained of the Empire, and the re-establishment of British influence in the Middle East, forced the Labour government to impose peacetime conscription in a form of 'national service'. As first planned in 1947 National Service was expected to require one year in the Armed Forces, but the recognition of the Cold War in Europe and concern about the Communist insurgency in Malaya meant that this year was immediately extended to eighteen months, and after the outbreak of the Korean War (1950-53) the period was again lengthened to two full years. As this conscription involved every physically fit young male over the age of 18, it gave the armed services access to men with a talent for learning languages who would not under normal peacetime conditions have been forthcoming.[3]

In the years 1942 to 1945 provision had already been made to give language training to young men who had completed their secondary school examinations and were awaiting call-up, and the Board of Education offered scholarships to selected schoolboys to attend special courses. The first batch of such men was housed in Dulwich College and attended the University of London's School of Oriental and African Studies (SOAS) to learn Japanese – Bletchley Park also ran its own intensive Japanese language courses – while the second group studied Russian and other Slavonic languages at SOAS's counterpart, the School of Slavonic and East European Studies (SSEES). The armed forces also made use of facilities at Cambridge University.[4] The Inter-Services Languages Committee, set up to coordinate the various language programmes, recommended that they should all be placed under the control of the Joint Intelligence Committee of Cabinet, and working parties on the training of Russian linguists and translators led to the establishment of the Joint Services School for Linguists (JSSL) in September 1951.[5]

The focus of languages used in intelligence work shifted as geopolitical realities changed. After the end of World War II German and Japanese lost their earlier importance, to be replaced by Russian and other Central and East European languages. Subsequent political developments led to the addition of Chinese (both Mandarin and Cantonese) to the mix. The programme of Chinese language instruction was carried on in parallel with Russian right up to the

4

early 1960s, both programmes being under the nominal umbrella of JSSL and operating in basically similar ways. Throughout their relatively short life span, however, the two were always organisationally autonomous, and only as the end of National Service approached were the services able to bring Russian and Chinese linguists physically together in the same camp (at Tangmere in Sussex). It is the story of the Chinese linguists in particular, their training and their contribution to the intelligence effort of Britain and its allies, that these pages now seek to tell.

* * * * * * * *

Fifty years on, it is not easy to recognise the world as it was viewed at that time. Britain and the world as a whole were still suffering the after-effects of World War II, and a brief history may help to set the scene at the time that the first National Servicemen to be trained as Chinese linguists were called up.

It was in 1955 that Winston Churchill resigned as Prime Minister, to be replaced by Sir Anthony Eden, while later in the same year Clement Attlee resigned as leader of the Labour Party opposition in Parliament, to be succeeded by Hugh Gaitskell. That year marked the birth of such later successful careerists as Tim Berners-Lee, the British inventor of the World Wide Web, Bill Gates and Steve Jobs who made fortunes from computer software, Sir Simon Rattle the orchestral conductor, film stars Kevin Costner and Whoopi Goldberg, Ian Botham the cricketer and Alain Prost the racing driver. No less notably, deaths in that year included those of Albert Einstein, Carmen Miranda, the jazz musician Charlie Parker and the teenage film idol James Dean. Back home, Britain was still enjoying the euphoria of 'the second Elizabethan age', and the Queen's firstborn Charles, now approaching seven years old, was soon to set a royal precedent by attending local day school.

The average wage in the United Kingdom was about £7-9 a week – though a month's wages would buy a functioning second-hand car, and a couple of thousand pounds would give access to a wide variety of quality housing in most parts of the country. But there were still shortages of many goods – meat rationing had only finally ended in 1954 – and the wartime philosophy of 'Make Do and Mend' was still prevalent. Steam trains, coal fires and smog in the cities were part of normal life, and a considerable number of families still lived in 'prefabs' – quick-build prefabricated houses put up by local councils on any spare bit of land. In leisure pursuits in 1955, the year in which linguists on the first RAF-run Chinese course for National Servicemen were called up, the first edition of the board game 'Scrabble' was introduced, the first edition of the Guinness Book of Records was published, and in America the original Disneyland opened in California.

In the diplomatic and military fields, a great deal was happening. In Europe, West Germany became a sovereign nation. Austria also regained its independence as the Allied troops left after a ten-year occupation, and the last prisoners from World War II were released by the Soviet Union. On the eastern edges of Europe eight Communist bloc countries signed the Warsaw Pact, and a nuclear bomb was tested in Siberia. Great Britain had tested its first atomic bomb in 1952, and continued tests at various sites in Australia throughout the 1950s. The British had largely abandoned any notion of Empire, but were in continuing conflict with the Mau Mau in Kenya, with EOKA terrorists in Cyprus, and – though it was not yet headline news – were becoming concerned about Colonel Nasser in Egypt and the future of the Suez Canal. The French were fighting a rearguard action against nationalists in Morocco and ruthlessly attempting to destroy similar uprisings in Algeria, after their final embarrassing withdrawal from Indo-China the previous year, and in the USA the Civil Rights movement was just getting under way.

In the Far East, the Korean War had ended in stalemate in 1953, leaving a long shadow which still remains. According to unofficial estimates around two million people lost their lives in that war, both civilians and military personnel, the latter including over one thousand British troops. The United States and China had found themselves in opposing camps, and although the most strident era of McCarthyism (during which hundreds of American politicians and personalities were accused of Communist sympathies) had passed, the United States was in the grip of an anti-Communist fear as potent as any panic about international terrorism in later years. A weak Europe, dependent on American defence systems, tended to acquiesce. The principal danger, in the eyes of Europe, was of course from the USSR, but from the point of view of the USA in the Western Pacific it was China which was seen as a much greater threat to international stability. As always, there was a long history behind this; a still recovering Japan was no longer a counter-balancing force to China, which had supported North Korea and had, or was thought to have, common interests with the Soviet Union against the West. (And, wheels within wheels, thorn-in-the-British-flesh Egypt was buying tanks from Communist bloc Czechoslovakia giving rise to fears that the Egyptians were slipping into the Soviet sphere of influence.) Chiang Kai-shek had fled from the Chinese mainland to Taiwan in 1949, where his Kuomintang government continued to be recognised by the United States as the legitimate Chinese state, rather than that of Chairman Mao's 'People's Republic of China' in Beijing. Britain's recognition of Mao's regime in 1950 was a source of irritation for the US government, which in 1954 signed a mutual defence pact with Taiwan.

As a consequence of this worldwide diplomatic and military turmoil, there was a sense of apprehension and patriotic commitment about National Service which allowed conscription to continue without any public opposition, despite the prevailing attitude that it was two years of a young man's life wasted. As one might imagine, the vast majority of the young men concerned knew little about the detail of international politics, and cared less, but accepted that there was no alternative, short of conscientious objection, but to do one's time in the armed forces before returning to civilian life. A few young men were excused Service on medical grounds, and as the years passed an increasingly large minority obtained deferment on the grounds of educational or training commitments. But for most conscripts it was customary to cross off the days on the calendar to see how long they still had to go till 'demob', the magic date of the prosaically named demobilisation, whilst those who had completed one year's service and thus were on the downward slope derisively urged new recruits to 'get some in'.

In the case of the trainee linguists, it seems that the sense of insulation from 'real life' felt by National Servicemen in general was enhanced by their further isolation from other parts of the internal world of the RAF. To some extent this feeling was deliberately fostered by the trainees themselves – after all, all the groups were tiny in military terms, and saw themselves as having been hand-picked – but there was an impression that this insularity was encouraged by the authorities. To begin with, all those who had been selected were required to sign the Official Secrets Act, as an extra gesture of patriotic dependability before they were allowed to enter the compound where the classrooms were located. Then, because during their training in Britain they spent daytime hours confined to their classrooms, and later in Hong Kong had fixed working shifts spread over the twenty-four hours, they were rarely involved in the usual spit and polish tasks other than basic housekeeping. Mostly they liked to think that they were above such chores, but the likelihood is that they were protected by their unit officers who controlled this miniature enclave in the armed forces where they had a great deal of personal responsibility for the outcome, and therefore a degree of independence. During the months of immersion in the Chinese language, most of these small course groups became closely bonded, with their allegiance being less to the United Kingdom or even to the RAF (despite disdain for the Army), and more to their own officer-instructors and to the group of colleagues with whom they spent, for the greater part of two years, at least as much time as boarding school boys would spend together. Hence the continuation of course reunions in later years by many of the members of individual course groups.

Notes

1   For more on the operations at Bletchley Park see Hinsley/ Stripp (1993) and Smith (1998). Smith (2000) deals with the breaking of Japanese codes during World War II. Keegan (2003), pp. 20-28, has a good summary of the nature and historical development of signals intelligence from the middle of the nineteenth century to the end of the twentieth.

2   Dorril (2000), p. 47.

3   The first armed forces Chinese course was held at the University of London's School of Oriental and African Studies (SOAS) in 1951-52, made up entirely of regular airmen on engagements of three years or longer. But the extension of the term of National Service from eighteen months to two years meant that there was now sufficient time to provide a full year of language training to conscripts, and on its completion to make some operational use of their newly acquired skills.

4   Elliott /Shukman (2002) and Lee (1999).

5   JSSL, sometimes also referred to as JSLS (Joint Services Language School), is discussed further in Chapter 2.

2

A DELICATE BUSINESS

'Espionage is a delicate business;
there is no situation in which it is not employed.'
(Sunzi, Art of War, 13.4)

During the 1950s and early 1960s selected National Service airmen spent a year at a base in Britain acquiring a knowledge of the elements of the spoken Chinese language, and then were posted to RAF Little Sai Wan in Hong Kong to perform voice intercept work at its outstations, Batty's Belvedere on the Peak and, to a very limited extent, Tai Mo Shan and Kong Wei in the New Territories.[1] That, in a sentence, summarises the theme of this book, and it also represents virtually everything that most of those airmen knew at the time, about what they were doing and in whose interests they were working. Servicemen are traditionally neither encouraged, nor indeed permitted, to ask unsolicited questions of their superiors, and this particularly applied to those who had, at the beginning of their training, been required to sign the Official Secrets Act, to the accompaniment of severe warnings that the smallest breach of its provisions would be met with dire consequences.

Accordingly these humble servants of the Queen passed their two years of compulsory service entirely within the confines of the Royal Air Force, which as far as they were concerned had been assigned the task of teaching them Chinese and was the main, possibly the sole, beneficiary of their work output. Occasionally one or two mysterious words or acronyms might escape the lips of their instructors and superior officers: some learned that they were (or would later be) engaged in SIGINT (Signals Intelligence) work, and a very few heard mention of a shadowy organisation known as GCHQ (Government Communications Headquarters) which, they were told, might even be able to make use of their services after they returned to civilian life.[2]

With the progressive declassification in recent years of once secret materials, and an increasing – if grudging – official willingness, if not to disclose the specific content, at least to admit to the existence and general nature of intelligence operations, a clearer picture of the place of Chinese linguists in the broader intelligence-gathering picture is beginning to emerge. Yet much uncertainty remains, for the intelligence community has always comprised what one commentator has aptly termed a 'myriad of organisations',[3] with functions that are not always precisely defined and often overlap one with another.

An attempt to unravel this organisational complexity might well start with GCHQ itself. Its predecessor, the Government Code & Cypher School (GC&CS), was established in October 1919,[4] and a major and justly renowned contribution was made to the success of the Allied war effort in World War II by the codebreakers, translators and analysts who worked under its aegis at Bletchley Park in Buckinghamshire, also known as 'Station X'. GC&CS was therefore, and GCHQ – as it became after a name change in 1946[5] – remains, the primary provider of SIGINT output to its consumers in Britain: to the Foreign Office under whose direct control it operates as a branch of the Civil Service,[6] and also, through the Joint Intelligence Committee (JIC) of Cabinet, to various ministers and to the Prime Minister of the day.[7] The interaction between GCHQ and the highest levels of government is no mere theoretical fiction; on a recent public occasion, two of the present authors were gratified to hear the current Director of GCHQ state that every morning throughout the Cold War years, thanks to the SIGINT material received and processed at GCHQ's central offices near Cheltenham, his predecessors were able personally to assure the Prime Minister of the day that global hostilities were unlikely to break out within the next twenty-four hours. It is also well established that during World War II Prime Minister Churchill himself took a lively interest in the activities carried on at Bletchley Park, recognising their critical importance for the war effort, and that on at least one occasion he was approached directly by codebreakers frustrated by unresponsive superiors, and made a forceful intervention on their behalf.[8]

It was therefore at the behest and for the eventual benefit of GCHQ that service linguists performed their tasks during the 1950s and 1960s. The three services, to the varying degrees that each was involved in such operations, merely provided the infrastructure, the personnel and the means of delivering the output of SIGINT to those who sought to make use of it. By and large, though the average service linguist might have been unaware of the fact, in its raw form none of this output was used by the branch of the armed forces generating it, and as a rule no attempt was made to do so. Transcripts of all the intercepts recorded at such places as Batty's Belvedere in Hong Kong were initially sent for analysis to GCHQ's Australian and American counterparts, the Defence Signals Division (DSD) and National Security Agency (NSA) respectively, organisations which will be described in greater detail later in this chapter. Reports compiled from the results of DSD and NSA's analysis were then forwarded to Cheltenham, and this material was added to the corpus of intelligence data assembled from a variety of sources, the monitoring of the military radio transmissions of potential adversaries being just one.[9] Indeed it was at one time claimed that 'the great bulk' of Britain's entire intelligence product passed through and emanated from GCHQ,[10] and with new responsibilities more recently added to its earlier functions, this estimate may well continue to hold true.

Most if not all of the RAF stations in various parts of the world engaged in radio intercept work during the Cold War years belonged to No. 90 Signals Group. But voice intercepts were but one of the several different types of signal with which the group was concerned. Placing stations within No. 90 Signals Group was therefore more a matter of administrative convenience than because all shared a common function.

From the perspective of GCHQ, however, stations such as Little Sai Wan and Batty's Belvedere were viewed in a very different organisational context. While Cheltenham was GCHQ's command centre, its mission was carried out by a chain of posts both military and civilian forming the 'Composite Signals Organisation' (CSO).[11] The CSO had been brought into existence in 1947 to replace the Y Service which played a corresponding role in the work of GC&CS.[12] The dual character of operational posts is illustrated by the fact that the RAF's 'No. 367 Signals Unit, Little Sai Wan' was identified by GCHQ, even when under direct military control, as 'Composite Signals Organisation Station Little Sai Wan' or as 'UKA 275A', its official designation in the international SIGINT network.[13]

One further general point needs to be made about GCHQ: it is not a division of the Secret Intelligence Service (SIS), popularly known as MI6. The links between the two bodies have always been quite tenuous, and became especially so after 1946, when the newly constituted GCHQ took over all SIGINT functions previously exercised by the SIS's Section R8.[14] This section was then reduced to a single liaison officer despatched once a week to the London office of GCHQ and once a month to Cheltenham.[15] While extensive intelligence operations were allegedly conducted by the SIS in Hong Kong in the post-war period, there is no evidence that these were ever connected to or coordinated with the SIGINT collection activities undertaken on behalf of GCHQ.

GCHQ did not evolve and grow throughout the Cold War years purely according to the dictates of the British government or the British military high command. It also forms part of a worldwide intelligence network comprising a number of countries with similar security concerns and similar political and strategic objectives.

Foremost among these is the United States, with Australia, Canada and New Zealand as partners alongside Britain. Norway, Denmark, the German Federal Republic and Turkey joined as 'third parties' after the formation of the network.[16]

All of these intelligence-sharing relationships have their origins in the so-called 'UKUSA Agreement' which provided, inter alia, for a division of the world for intelligence gathering purposes into zones of national responsibility.[17] However Hong Kong's place in the grand scheme created by the UKUSA Agreement was always slightly anomalous. On paper the whole of the western Pacific fell within the American sphere of responsibility, but it made sense (diplomatic sense perhaps, if not strategically) that the British should continue to be responsible for intelligence gathering in territories under their direct political control. A further complication resulted however from the fact that under an earlier Commonwealth SIGINT Agreement, Hong Kong had been designated as part of Australia's geographical area of responsibility.[18] Thus throughout its years of operation, according to most sources, Little Sai Wan technically fell within the exclusive jurisdiction of the Defence Signals Division (DSD), the Australian counterpart to GCHQ.[19] At the same time, while it may have been home to a contingent of Australian service personnel furnished by that country's Directorate of Air Force Intelligence which varied in size over time (and occasionally also to a number of New Zealanders),[20] British servicemen always made up the bulk of its strength, and the officers commanding both the station itself and the signals unit within it were invariably drawn from the RAF. Only the outpost of Batty's Belvedere, for the first few years after its establishment, came under the command of an Australian officer, Bill Barber.[21]

The DSD of the 1950s was later renamed the Defence Signals Branch (DSB), and later still reverted to its original initials as the Defence Signals Directorate. The reasons for and the practical consequences of these changes remain unclear, and they are not in any case particularly relevant to our story. As mentioned above, transcripts of all intercepts made at Little Sai Wan and Batty's Belvedere were sent in the first instance to DSD headquarters in Melbourne; only afterwards did GCHQ receive reports based on the analysis of these transcripts by DSD. The length of time between receipt of the transcripts in Melbourne and receipt of the intelligence reports in Cheltenham is uncertain – it may indeed have varied – nor do we know whether all of the information garnered from the transcripts was incorporated into the reports, or merely such information as DSD considered to be militarily significant. Until the Australian authorities show the same readiness as the British to grant access to once secret documents, these questions must remain unanswered.

It is however known that the entire SIGINT output from Hong Kong found its way to the headquarters of GCHQ's American counterpart organisation, the National Security Agency (NSA), at Fort Meade between Baltimore and Washington.[22] It is also clear that in intelligence-gathering matters the dictates of the NSA were paramount. No less a figure than the deputy chief of the SIS in the late 1950s and early 1960s went on record as saying that in the technical field GCHQ had been reduced to an 'ancillary branch' of the NSA.[23] One wonders, however, whether the allegation might have been prompted by a certain measure of inter-agency rivalry and malice, since SIS had quite recently been forced to cede its remaining SIGINT functions to GCHQ. According to another source, in 1952 the NSA, possibly responding to concerns expressed two years earlier by then Secretary of State Dean Acheson, urged the British government to accept the offer of an eight hundred-strong US Air Force unit to help out the 'hard-pressed' British and Australians in the intelligence field in Hong Kong.[24] Given the United States's known shortage of Chinese interpreters to meet the needs of their forces serving in Korea at that time,[25] it is inconceivable that more than a few of the personnel included in this offer would have been linguists. In any event the offer was never taken up, and over the next few years British SIGINT capability in Hong Kong grew rapidly, so that the need for American assistance no longer arose. The proposal, while illustrative of the dominance in the intelligence field which the Americans already exercised, may have been put forward for no other reason than to spur the British and Australian authorities into making that very increase in SIGINT capability. All important communications between the United States and Britain on matters of this nature were routed through the Technical Radio Intercept Committee (TRIC), a joint body set up in the wake of the UKUSA Agreement to provide liaison between their respective intelligence services.[26] Other channels of communication included the Special US Liaison Office (SUSLO), established in 1952 with offices in the United States Embassy in London and in GCHQ at Cheltenham, and its counterpart the Special UK Liaison Office (SUKLO) inside NSA headquarters at Fort Meade.[27]

Though not directly relevant to our theme, it is of interest to note that the rivalries between the transatlantic allies in the intelligence field were for a time reflected at the diplomatic and administrative levels in Hong Kong. Relations between the British and United States governments and their respective intelligence agencies had already come under strain following the defection to the Soviet Union, in 1951, of SIS agents Guy Burgess and Donald Maclean.[28] A few years later the United States Consulate in Hong Kong, regarded at that time as one of the largest American diplomatic missions anywhere in the world, was found to be involved in wide-ranging espionage activities whose flagrant nature caused much annoyance and embarrassment to the British authorities, and prompted the colony's long-serving governor, Sir Alexander Grantham, to order the impounding of aircraft belonging to Civil Air Transport, the CIA's private arline.[29] But in this case the toes trodden on by the Americans would have been those of SIS and SIS alone, and it is quite possible that the affair was never officially brought to the attention of GCHQ and its officers in Hong Kong, since SIS operations there and elsewhere in the world were supposed to be completely insulated from contact with any part of the international SIGINT network.

Aside from the national and international structures governing SIGINT activity in the postwar period, it is also useful to place

16

the various operations at ground level in Hong Kong in their military administrative context. Despite its formal designation as a 'Composite Signals Organisation Station',[30] Little Sai Wan, situated beside a small bay at the eastern end of Hong Kong island, functioned as a regular – if slightly unorthodox and by military standards mildly sybaritic – RAF station, with the usual physical apparatus of guardroom, messes for officers and NCOs, airmen's dining hall, NAAFI,[31] administrative, educational and medical blocks, barrack rooms and so forth. Here almost all of the Chinese linguists were housed for the duration of their tours of duty, sharing quarters with a much larger group of wireless operators (W/Ops, who intercepted telegraphic transmissions) and a handful of members of other trades.[32]

One building at Little Sai Wan, not mentioned in the foregoing list, was the Technical Block, staffed mainly by W/Ops plying their trade, and by NCOs and officers engaged in the monitoring and analysis of SIGINT. Here was to be found the 'nerve centre' of this important link in the international SIGINT network, while in RAF terms the Technical Block was the heart and hub of No. 367 Signals Unit (367 SU); the Australians for their part treated it as the operational base of a detachment of 3TelU (No. 3 Telecommunications Unit), headquartered at RAAF Pearce in Western Australia. Other SIGINT-gathering locations in Hong Kong, such as Batty's Belvedere and its outposts at Tai Mo Shan and Kong Wei in the New Territories, were viewed in the service structure as component parts of 367 SU, and fell within the jurisdiction of that unit's commanding officer, who usually held the same rank as the station commanding officer. It was widely believed, though never authenticated, that most if not all of the station commanding officers at Little Sai Wan lacked the security clearance needed to enter the Technical Block, and had to defer to the officer commanding 367 SU over all questions related to its operations. Batty's Belvedere had its own commanding officer, but he was normally a rank or two lower than the other two, and it is a reasonable supposition, though no more than that, that given the subordinate position of Batty's its entire SIGINT output made its way in the first instance to the Technical Block at Little Sai Wan before being sent on to Melbourne and Fort Meade with the rest of the material from Hong Kong.

To complete this brief tour of the actual, if at the time largely invisible, world which the Chinese linguists inhabited during their two years of service, attention should be directed for a moment away from the complexities of the intelligence apparatus to the curious structure that had formal responsibility for all language training in the armed forces. Since all three services were to a greater or lesser extent involved in this field, an umbrella organisation was created, allegedly under direct orders from 10 Downing Street,[33] to coordinate their respective endeavours. This was the Joint Services School for Linguists (JSSL), later sometimes called the Joint Services Language School (JSLS).[34] Most accounts attribute a life span of around ten years to JSSL, from 1951 to 1960, but even after the ending of conscription it appears to have survived in a truncated form to provide courses both for servicemen (in languages other than Chinese) and for civilian trainees in the employ of GCHQ.[35] During the earlier years of its existence the school conducted its activities in a variety of service establishments, offering basic Russian language courses at Bodmin in Cornwall and later at Crail in eastern Scotland, while technical training was carried out at Wythall near Birmingham and (from 1957 to 1959) at Pucklechurch near Bristol. Its Russian and Chinese components operated as separate and functionally independent units right up to 1959, when Tangmere in Sussex became the single centre for all instruction, both basic and technical, in all of the languages then offered by JSSL. Until this came about there was little if any significant contact between the staffs and student bodies of the two elements, and many pre-1959 trainee linguists on the Chinese side, if they had heard the name of JSSL at all, assumed that it was responsible solely for the provision of Russian courses, and certainly did not include themselves.

Did the school have an administrative headquarters away from the training centres, and to what higher body was it accountable for the proper performance of its functions? For the moment the answers to these questions remain unclear, but it may well have reported directly to the Joint Intelligence Committee of Cabinet (JIC), with this committee setting out policies for it and passing along to JSSL the requirements of GCHQ which was another of the JIC's reporting agencies.[36] Recently declassified documents suggest that the Air Ministry (and no doubt the same was true for the War Office and the Admiralty) had little if any involvement with the day-to-day workings of JSSL; the main ongoing concern of its Language Training Planning Committee was to determine the number of linguists that would be required a year or two hence for operational duties in Hong Kong and other SIGINT centres. Nevertheless, as will be shown in the next chapter, it played an important role in setting standards for the recruitment and training of service linguists and interpreters.[37]

Notes

1   Mirsky (1980) and 367/7.4. Brief descriptions of the ambiance and operations of a typical intercept post may be found in Elliott/Shukman (2003), pp. 8-9 and 185; see also Campbell (2000).

2   Three members of No. 6 Course were in fact seconded to GCHQ in Cheltenham on completion of their twelve months of language training. Since these men had only a short time remaining in their two years of National Service, it was not considered worthwhile sending them out to Hong Kong for operational duties there. Information supplied by Lawrie Cooke.

3   Bennett/Bennett (2003).

4   West (1986), p. 73.

5   Officially in 1946: Smith (1998), p. 226; but it seems that

by then the name was already being used unofficially as a cover for GC&CS activities: Dorril (2000), p. 56.

6   Aldrich (1998), p. 2.

7   Bennett/Bennett (2003).

8   Bennett/Bennett (2003); Macksey (2003), pp. 131-132.

9   Elliott/Shukman (2003), p. 177.

10   Campbell/Kane (1980), p. 738. More recently it has been estimated that 'more than 70% of all the intelligence gathered in the UK' is generated by GCHQ: Bennett/Bennett (2003).

11   Campbell (2000).

12   Bennett/Bennett (2003).

13   After GCHQ assumed direct control over operations at Little Sai Wan, the station's SIGINT designation was changed to UKC 201.

14   Davies (2004), p. 187; Smith (1998), p. 226.

15   Davies (2004), p. 189. Peter Wright, a former GCHQ 'insider', claimed that by 1955 the Cheltenham meetings were taking place only once every six months: Wright (1987), p. 79.

16   Campbell (2000).

17   Minnick (2003). Minnick, Richelson and Ball (1985), p. 6 and West (1988), p. 260 cite 1947 as the year in which the agreement was concluded, while other writers date it to

1948: Aldrich (1998), pp. 43-44; Campbell (2000); Dorril (2000), pp. 52, 56. Both 1946 and 1948 (June) appear in Bennett/Bennett (2003); 1946 is also preferred by Bamford (2001), p. 394 and Smith (1998), p. 278. The uncertainty over the date may be attributable to the fact that the UKUSA Agreement remains, even now, a 'highly secret agreement'; Bamford (2001), p. 403.

18   Ball (1996), p. 480. West (1986), p. 205, claims that the SIGINT world had already been 'carved up' between the countries concerned in November 1943, several years before the signing of the UKUSA Agreement.

19   Ball (1996), p. 481. Ball (1996), pp. 477-478, and Campbell/ Kane (1980), p. 739, refer to Little Sai Wan as a joint GCHQ/ DSD operation. Aldrich (2001), p. 308, makes the curious observation that it was run jointly by the British, Americans and Australians.

20   West (1986), p. 223; West (1988), p. 259. David Iliff, who worked at Batty's Belvedere in 1959-60, recalls that the initial analysis of intercepts was carried out by Australians.

21   367/2.10 and 367/6.53.

22   Aldrich (2001), p. 400; Elliott/Shukman (2003), p. 189.

23   Dorril (2000), p. 650.

24   Aldrich (2001), p. 400.

25   Summers (1990), p. 185.

26   Aldrich (1998), pp. 47-48.

27   Bennett/Bennett (2003); Campbell (2000). SUSLOs were also posted to Canberra and Wellington: Bamford (2001), p. 498.

28   Wright (1987), pp. 98-99; Keegan (2003), p. 386. Keegan maintains that 'for a long time [afterwards] the Americans took the view that the British intelligence services were fundamentally flawed if not corrupt.'

29   Aldrich (2001), pp. 311-312. Civil Air Transport had its operational base in Taiwan: Minnick (2003), but its aircraft were frequently to be seen parked on the apron at Kai Tak in the 1950s.

30   Ball (1996), p. 477.

31   Navy, Army and Air Force Institutes, an organisation technically independent of the Armed Forces which ran (and continues to run) recreational facilities and food service establishments for service personnel and their families. See *www.naafi.co.uk.*

32   While initially 367 SU occupied a number of different locations in Hong Kong, from 1951 onwards Little Sai Wan served at its operational headquarters until the civilianisation of intelligence work in 1962: Ball (1996), p. 477.

33   Elliott/Shukman (2003), p. 34.

34   Since it is difficult to establish the precise date on which JSSL officially became JSLS, for simplicity's sake the abbreviation JSSL is used exclusively throughout this book.

35   For some ten years prior to its disbandment in 1997 a successor organisation known as CATS (Communications

Analysis Training School) performed a function similar to that of JSSL/JSLS.

36   Elliott/Shukman (2003), pp. 36-38.

37   See for example the minutes of an Air Ministry meeting on 16 October 1953, AIR 2/11394 (RAF Personnel: Regular and National Service Entrants Selected for Training in Foreign Languages, Arrangements for Selection, Training and Conditions of Service).

3

MANDARINS IN WHITEHALL

*'This I am sure of: if her Majesty would have spent
but 1,000 crowns to have had some intelligence,
it would have saved her twenty times as much.'*

*(Charles Howard, Lord Effingham, Admiral of the English
Fleet to Sir Francis Walsingham, 24 January 1587)[1]*

On examination of the relevant files now available at the National
Archives[2] it becomes clear that in the 1950s and 1960s the War
Office, and then its successor, the Ministry of Defence (MoD),
discussed over a long period of time the question of the Joint
Services Language School (JSLS) and the functions of Linguists.
Originally set up as the Joint Services School of Linguists (JSSL)
at the beginning of the 1950s, mainly for training Russian linguists
at camps based in Bodmin and later Crail in Scotland, the title of
this organisation was later changed to the Joint Services Language
School. In August 1956, a Services Languages Training Committee,
chaired by an MoD representative, met several times in Whitehall
to discuss the use of 'Linguists in Voice Interception'. Within the
time frame of the RAF Chinese language programme, this was just
when members of No. 1 Course had almost completed their one year
of training, and members of No. 2 Course were five months into
theirs. During its deliberations the committee decided to expand its
classification of Linguists into four main categories:

1. Interpreter 1st class
2. Interpreter 2nd class
3. Linguist – Higher Grade
4. Linguist – Lower Grade

Subsequent minutes indicate a degree of disagreement between the Armed Services over these four classifications. The Army wished to amalgamate the two classes of Interpreter, while the Admiralty wanted to keep them separate. For lower grade Linguists the Army required them to have an oral capability only, whereas the Air Ministry insisted they should be able to read and write their chosen language; in fact this did not apply in the case of Chinese courses where the emphasis was on oral/aural skills, and the reading and writing of Chinese characters was not an official requirement. The following year, 1957, whether by accident or design, the MoD seemed to deal with differing inter-service priorities by creating a new executive body named the 'Services Language Policy Committee' under the leadership of the MoD, its terms of reference being 'to consider questions of policy relating to the requirements for and methods of language training in the Services'. The Services Language Training Committee, consisting of representatives of the Armed Services and GCHQ only, was now subordinate to the Policy Committee, to the extent that their modified terms of reference included the sentence: 'Matters on which there is disagreement and which cannot be resolved by the Committee will be referred to the Services Language Policy Committee.'

There was the constant thread of thinking throughout the committee meeting minutes recorded in the MoD files that Interpreters should be commissioned officers while Linguists would be Other Ranks. No. 1 Course had personal experience of these basic classifications at the beginning of their training. When the 39 National Service trainees started their programme at RAF Wythall in September 1955, they had three weeks of intensive study of Chinese, with weekly progress tests, followed by a language assessment test. Then each of them was individually interviewed by an officer selection board, and as a result of the test and interviews 15 of the group were selected to become Officer Cadets (Interpreter) and were transferred to a fulltime course of study at the School of Oriental & African Studies, London University, for the rest of their service. This left 24 of the original group at Wythall to continue their year-long language course there before being posted to Hong Kong. Several of the other ten Chinese Courses experienced this process of siphoning off officer cadets early on, but never in such a large number as No. 1 Course. This was presumably a sensible RAF investment to create a pool of Chinese interpreters to cover contingencies in the event of future hostilities.

Another interesting point arising from these meetings was that the committee noted that, while National Servicemen were necessary for national mobilisation requirements, they could not contribute so much to their linguist duties of voice interception, because after one year's training there was little time left in their two years of service. The committee felt that training National Servicemen was unnecessarily expensive in terms of value for money, and these funds could be used more profitably in other ways. However there was a general acceptance that it would not be possible to recruit such numbers of linguists, who were at the required level to undertake serious language training, from the pool of regular airmen only. In retrospect it seems fortunate for the peace of mind of all the Chinese linguists on the eleven courses from 1955 to 1962 that they had no idea of the existence of this committee or its musings on the costs of language training. They were able to plough on with their language learning in blissful ignorance because the committee never implemented any cost-cutting action against the Language School, the implication being that the three Armed Services were in principle supporting the recruitment of National Servicemen for the JSLS. However with the end of National Service looming, the decision was made to civilianise the work of the RAF linguists, and so the responsibility for training Chinese speakers, and most of the associated costs, devolved upon GCHQ. This change had taken place by the time the members of No 11 Chinese course (the last one) were demobilised in November 1962, but in fact even after that several RAF Officers continued to teach on the Chinese language programme until replaced by civilian teachers. As for native Chinese instructors, one of them, who started teaching No. 1 Course in 1955, was still on the staff of the Languages School at North Luffenham in 1969.

The work of the Services Language Training Committee in the 1950s covered the three Armed Services, which between them required foreign language speakers or voice intercepters in many languages. The committee divided this wide range of languages into three main groups although it is not known what criteria were used in this classification process; and in fact languages could be re-allocated between the different groups at any time. For example some languages, such as Arabic, Ghurkali, Malay and Swahili, were deemed 'theatre' languages because of military involvement in particular parts of the world, but in reality there was also the need to facilitate international military communications and liaison with allies and other nations, and to provide service attaches who could be posted to key British Embassies worldwide and who were proficient in those languages. As is made clear in a later document, not only was there intelligence gathering from so-called enemy or unfriendly nations, but in addition Cold War espionage included clandestine monitoring of the communications of allied and friendly countries.[3] To give some idea of the scope of languages covered, according to the committee minutes, the Army had the largest need for officers with language qualifications, totalling forty-four different languages ranging alphabetically from Afrikaans to West African, while the Royal Navy required personnel to cover nineteen languages ranging from Arabic to Turkish. The Royal Air Force had the smallest requirement, consisting of the following twelve languages: Arabic, Chinese, Czech, French, German, Greek, Hebrew, Italian, Polish, Portuguese, Russian and Spanish. Of these languages, Arabic, Chinese and Russian speakers were in greatest demand.

This leads on to the composition of the Group I list of languages, which were Arabic, Chinese, Japanese, Russian, Persian, Siamese,

Turkish. It is probable that the committee regarded these languages as difficult to learn, although some of the Group II languages such as Amharic, Burmese, Hebrew, Hungarian, Finnish and Korean could equally well have been included in Group I. Group III languages were Western European and Scandinavian so they must have represented 'easier' languages, as well as being the languages of the UK's allies or friendly countries. Nevertheless the committee minutes revealed that Arabic, Chinese and Russian were together regarded as key target languages and as the three most difficult languages to learn. To recruit suitable personnel for language training, the committee was continually grappling with the problem of the embedded career disincentive that habitually inhibited commissioned officers from applying for language qualifications, i.e. they would have no proper RAF role outside of their language duties. The committee did not want short service officers who were solely language specialists, rather it preferred someone with a service background who could also speak a language. To illustrate its attitude, when discussing suitable financial inducements to persuade commissioned officers to choose language training courses, the committee produced a table of financial awards rising through four levels of language proficiency: Colloquial--Linguist--Interpreter (2nd class)-- Interpreter (1st class). 'Colloquial' was an additional category that suddenly appeared in the minutes out of the blue, and there was no information given there to help assess its status and definition, and how it related to Linguist grade. Suffice it to say that it was bottom of any table of awards, the top inducements being for Interpreters of the three key languages, £180 for Chinese and £90 for Arabic and Russian. Of course this table of awards only referred to regular service personnel and did not apply to National Servicemen!

In April 1957 the Service Language Training Committee, under the umbrella of the MoD, issued a sixteen page confidential document entitled 'Language Training in the Services' which summarised the realities of its continuous deliberations, the final pages being a 'Definition of the Linguist Standard'. This should be of interest to all Service personnel who trained on language courses in the post-war period, and became Interpreters or Linguists.

28

DEFINITION OF THE LINGUIST STANDARD

Precise definition of a standard to be reached in a language is extremely difficult if not impossible. All that can be done is to suggest considerations which indicate a standard. The following should indicate to examining bodies and to teachers of languages what is meant by the Linguist Standard:

a)   The Linguist standard should be reached after about half the time taken to reach Interpreter standard. The time taken to reach Interpreter standard varies according to the difficulty of the language. With Russian, for example, an officer with an aptitude for languages should reach Linguist standard after about a ten months' full-time course.

b)   The knowledge of the language in structure, grammar and general vocabulary should be up to Advanced level of the G.C.E.[4] But the Linguist will not be required to have the literary background needed for the G.C.E. The Linguist's training will be for functional service uses. He should not be expected to have an analytical knowledge of the language nor to command its finer subtleties.

c)   The Linguist should be able to translate the sense of all general service material into English both from writing and from speech(including recordings). He should be able to understand most of what appears in the popular vernacular Press and to get the main sense from a general broadcast talk.

d)   The Linguist should be competent to perform all simple oral liaison tasks in the foreign language. He should be able to establish a working arrangement with his foreign counterpart which will allow both of them to co-operate with understanding in joint undertakings.

e)   The Interpreter is expected to translate spontaneously with precision of word, phrase and idiom. The Linguist will not have to be so quick in his linguistic reaction. He will not be so much a translator as an interpreter of meaning. His more limited knowledge of the language will cause him to be slower, since he will be searching within this limited knowledge to find language which will communicate the main sense and meaning of what he hears. However, the main strength of the Linguist will reside in his oral fluency and aural comprehension.

This definition seems eminently reasonable, and gives some idea of the language skills needed for the services in those times. It is as well to remember that the training for all languages that were not included in the curriculum of secondary schools would have to start from scratch, so much credit should be given to the teachers and the teaching of these languages. One can only guess as to how this definition of a linguist would relate to the criteria used today in the selection of service linguists. For example, information to the wider public is freely available today on the RAF careers website for the recruitment of Intelligent Analysts, a more sophisticated version of what the National Service linguists did:

> Intelligence Analysts (Voice) listen to, monitor and analyse radio messages that are broadcast throughout the world. You'll operate a wide variety of state-of-the-art receiving and recording systems, specialising in voice communications. To do your work you'll undertake a long and challenging training course, graduating as a linguist in a modern language. ....For security reasons, details of the work you'll do are restricted, but you'll need a high standard of hearing and security clearance is required.[5]

There is no mention of which languages are involved, but on looking at the twelve languages pinpointed by the RAF in the 1950s, nine were European (including Russian), two were Middle Eastern, and the other Chinese; not exactly a worldwide spread. In the light of the current threat posed by international terrorism it seems to safe to assume that a wider range of global languages, or even dialects, has now been added to the list to be covered by UK security bodies for intelligence-gathering purposes. There must be a considerable number of language classes taking place in hidden classrooms in the UK today, involving more languages than in the days of Chinese linguists during the Cold War period in the 1950s.

Notes

1   From John Langton, *Defeat of the Spanish Armada, Anno 1588* (2 vols., London: Naval Research Society, 1894), 1.46.

More recently the same quotation has been used by Robert Hutchinson to introduce, on page 203, chapter 7 of his excellent biographical study of Francis Walsingham entitled *Elizabeth's Spy Master* (London: Weidenfeld & Nicolson, 2006).

2   All material referred to or quoted in this chapter, other than the citations in notes 1, 3, 4 and 5, comes from file DEFE 10/343 (Services Language Training Committee: Minutes of Meetings and Memoranda, 1956-1958 and Services Language Policy Committee: Minutes of Meetings and Memoranda, 1958-1962) in the National Archives.

3   Ramparts Magazine (1972).

4   G.C.E.: the General Certificate of Education examination which could be taken at age sixteen, at the end of compulsory secondary education.

5   RAF Careers website: *www.raf.mod.uk/careers*.

4

A MATTER OF ORGANISATION

'Managing men, whether many or few, is
simply a matter of organisation.'
(Sunzi, Art of War, 5.1)

In 1951, when the first group of airmen had been selected to learn Chinese, they were posted to the RAF station at Uxbridge, just outside London. Uxbridge had played a prominent part in the Battle of Britain, but after World War II it ceased to be a centre of flying operations, instead extending its hospitality to such diverse elements as military bandsmen and the ground troops of the RAF Regiment. Its martial atmosphere was hardly conducive to intellectual pursuits, but the future Chinese linguists would not be receiving their instruction there – that was to be the role of the University of London's School of Oriental and African Studies (SOAS), located in Russell Square. SOAS had had a long history of success in practical language training, chiefly for the Foreign and Colonial Offices, and it therefore seemed a natural choice for this new assignment.

So it was decided by the planners at the Air Ministry that the trainee Chinese linguists would merely live at the Uxbridge base, and that each working day they would don civilian clothes (either a service issue suit or, more often as it turned out, something more stylish of their own choosing) and take the underground into SOAS in the morning, and back again to Uxbridge in the evening. For the most part Uxbridge served as little more than their dormitory, although their privileged status there did not afford them a complete escape from the serviceman's time-honoured routine; there were still station parades with the customary attendant bull, guard duties fell to their lot from time to time, and spit-and-polish NCOs (one corporal in particular is remembered, not too kindly, by some of the linguists) took it upon themselves to try to instil a little military discipline into men who, when they began their training, still held the lowest rank of AC 2.

The RAF's decision to rely solely on SOAS for its teaching expertise is of particular interest because a different pattern had already been established for Russian language training, which was carried out, and would continue to be carried out under the aegis of JSSL, using both service and native Russian instructors. While the RAF was involved to a certain degree in the operation of the Russian programme, the leading role in it had been assigned to the Royal Navy, with its longer history of interception of military wireless transmissions.[1] A few more years would elapse before a similar model was adopted for the Chinese language component of JSSL, with the RAF assuming sole responsibility for its conduct, though for what reasons the links with SOAS were then largely (though by no means completely) severed is unclear from the available source material. Certainly no hint of criticism, either of the standards at SOAS or of its teaching methods, is to be found. The courses which service students took there were under the general direction of Walter Simon, then Professor of Chinese at the University of London, and were conducted by his son Harry Simon, later appointed to and for many years occupant of the chair of Chinese at Melbourne University, as well as by other regular members of the SOAS teaching staff, including such distinguished sinologists as Cyril Birch, Göran Malmqvist,[2] James Y. Liu,[3] Gordon Downer, John Chinnery,[4] Angus C. Graham, Patrick D. Hanan,[5] D.C. Lau,[6] Mrs Yin Chi Liu (known to and highly regarded by several generations of Chinese language students)[7] and her sister Mrs Manning.[8]

The service students at SOAS (all regular airmen in the first intake, but mainly National Servicemen thereafter) took courses crafted to meet their specific needs, with greater emphasis on military and technical terminology, though a place was also found in the syllabus for the study of Chinese characters. Before long, however, they were joined at the school by other RAF personnel who sat in on the regular undergraduate lectures and classes. This second group consisted of regular officers, Squadron Leaders and Flight Lieutenants, several of them with distinguished war records in Fighter and Bomber Commands, who had now been assigned the task of learning Chinese so that they could act as directors and instructors for the courses which would later be run by the RAF alone, without SOAS participation. Their number included John Wright, the director of in-service Chinese language training from 1955 to 1959, Bennie Piff, a course director and instructor in 1956, Paddy (P.J.W.) Raine, a course director and instructor from 1957 to 1960, Ken Sly, a course director and instructor during the language school's later transition to a civilian operation,[9] and Harry Chandler, who is not known to have acted as an instructor but was on operational duty in Hong Kong in the mid-1950s. After their year at SOAS all these officers were sent on to Hong Kong University for a further two years of language study. During the same period another officer, Don Flint, was assigned the task of learning Cantonese rather than Mandarin, but by the time that he finished his studies at SOAS and Hong Kong University the Air Ministry had already concluded that its need for Cantonese linguists was diminishing,[10] and upon leaving SOAS he simply returned to his previous work in the engineering branch of the service.[11] (Some of the airmen selected for language training before 1953 took Cantonese rather than Mandarin courses – their instructors included Dr Katherine P. K. Whitaker who is remembered with affection and respect; but once it became clear that the Chinese armed forces were increasingly relying on Mandarin as their principal medium of communication, most of the Cantonese linguists – including some who had already served a tour in Hong Kong, but were not yet due for discharge – were sent back to SOAS for retraining.)[12]

A third group of RAF personnel taking courses at SOAS during this period should also be mentioned here. In 1953 nine students passed an Air Ministry selection board and were thereafter to continue their studies as officer cadets, with the prospect of receiving commissions in the Royal Air Force Volunteer Reserve (RAFVR) on completion of their term of active service. Their new status was confirmed when they moved from their relatively spartan quarters at Uxbridge to HMS President, an elegant if slightly faded hall of residence for JSSL officer cadets in much more prestigious surroundings, behind the Royal Albert Hall in South Kensington. At SOAS they took courses from the same lecturers as their officer and airman counterparts, courses which for some reason a few 'outsiders' were also permitted to attend, including most notably the pseudonymous Gordon Lonsdale who would later be unmasked as a Soviet spy. During the university vacations, the cadets were usually sent off to an RAF camp to live in the officers' mess and observe station activities, and shortly before the end of their studies at SOAS they were required to spend two weeks at Booker, near High Wycombe, completing a reserve officer training course which some recall as not having been too rigorous or demanding. Even after the RAF began to run its own Chinese language programme, the practice of choosing a number of airmen as officer cadets and sending them to SOAS for the balance of their National Service was continued intermittently: fifteen such students were selected from No. 1 Course, and three each from No. 3 and No. 5 Course.[13]

But the majority of service trainees at SOAS during these early years were airmen destined for service in Hong Kong. After spending at least nine months commuting from Uxbridge to their Chinese classes[14] they then proceeded to RAF Wythall, just south of Birmingham, for up to a month of technical training before being posted to Hong Kong.[15] This station had come into existence at the beginning of World War II, as the headquarters of No. 6 Balloon Centre, with responsibility for maintaining the barrage balloon defence of the Birmingham area. After the war ended it became, for a while, the WAAF (Women's Auxiliary Air Force) demobilisation centre, and then, until 1949, the No. 1 School of Administrative Trades. After a brief closure it was reactivated in 1952 and designated as an 'Applied Language School', serving all three armed forces; but little thought seems to have been given to the security implications of the sensitive activities to be carried on there, for in that year the newly appointed Station Commanding Officer, Wing Commander T.W. Hodgson, felt moved to communicate to his superiors his concern that 'a special school of the secret nature of the Applied Language School [is] sited here, where two civilian firms are to be allowed to continue to operate within a few yards of the school.'[16]

At first the Applied Language School at Wythall catered almost exclusively to Russian language students. Here they were given their technical training before going on assignment, with most of them receiving postings to bases close to the Iron Curtain in West Germany.[17] Three years later the scope of Wythall's involvement in the language field was enlarged when the authorities decided that future students of Chinese (or those, at any rate, who were destined for operational duty in Hong Kong) would no longer be taught the fundamentals of the language at SOAS; instead they would receive the necessary instruction at the RAF's own Applied Language School, to be delivered not by university lecturers but by serving officers and NCOs and by native Chinese instructors.[18]

For what reasons was this decision taken? Until more official documents are opened for public scrutiny we can only speculate, but it is not difficult to think of possible arguments in its favour. As suggested earlier, it is unlikely that dissatisfaction with the quality of teaching at SOAS was one of them. There may have been considerations of cost, although we have no information about the financial arrangements in place between the Air Ministry and SOAS during the period from 1951 to 1955. There may have been a wish to make the role of JSSL in language training more central, and to impose a greater degree of uniformity upon the structure and practices of its Russian and Chinese elements; or the RAF may simply have realised that SOAS would be unable to cope with the increasing numbers of service students who were now being selected for language training. At the same time, by organizing its

36

own courses it could ensure that the content of these courses more closely reflected operational needs, and making use as instructors of officers and NCOs who had recently returned from Hong Kong helped to solve a problem that was openly acknowledged by the Air Ministry: how to keep regular personnel who had completed their tours of duty overseas usefully occupied during the months that they were entitled to spend back home in Britain.[19]

The start of the RAF's direct involvement in teaching Chinese can be precisely dated, for it was on 5 September 1955 that John Wright, who had been appointed first director of the programme, arrived at Wythall after spending the previous few months touring recruit training camps to meet with prospective students.[20] Some 39 recently called-up National Servicemen had been selected for the first course (now officially designated No. 1) through a process which will be described in greater detail in chapter 7, and at the end of September they assembled at Wythall to begin almost a full year of intensive language training.

Thus was established a pattern of courses which continued throughout the RAF's six years of involvement with Chinese language teaching. For reasons related to staffing requirements in Hong Kong, as well as the National Serviceman's relatively short term of service, new courses would begin at approximately six-month intervals, and so it was that another twenty-nine airmen arrived at Wythall in early April 1956 to embark on the study of spoken Mandarin. Unlike No. 1 Course, which was composed entirely of conscripted airmen, No. 2 Course included four regular Army personnel: a staff sergeant, a corporal, a lance-corporal and a private.[21] It is not known how they subsequently made use of their knowledge of Chinese, though some or all of them may have been attached to Army units in Hong Kong; but their presence serves as a useful reminder that, although the RAF had been given exclusive responsibility for training Chinese linguists, the courses it offered were still technically under the aegis of JSSL, and we again find Army students participating in at least two of the later courses (Nos. 8 and 11).[22]

By mid-1956 Wythall found itself unable to accommodate all of the airmen who, for different reasons, had been posted there, and it was the fledging Chinese language programme which, in order to ease the overcrowding, received instructions to relocate. No. 1 Course was due to be completed in September and could stay at Wythall until then, but in July 1956, after their first leave, members of No. 2 Course were told to report to the tiny camp at Worth Matravers, near to the Dorset coast.[23] The main, and arguably the only, claim to fame of RAF Worth Matravers rested on the pioneering radar experiments conducted there in the early 1940s by Sir Robert Watson-Watt, the wartime head of the government's Radio Research Station, assisted by such future scientific luminaries as Sir Bernard Lovell. In the mid-1950s several of Watson-Watt's wooden towers, some thirty to forty feet in height, were still visible at Worth Matravers, but after its closure the entire camp was ploughed under, and today not a single trace of the site's military past remains.[24]

If the move from Wythall to Worth Matravers is of relatively slight importance in the broader picture, it is worth lingering over for a moment more, if only because it illustrates well the capricious nature of the documents which have survived and are approved for public release, and which now constitute the main official source for this history. More often than not one will search in vain through those documents for the minutes of meetings at which were discussed such important issues as the decision to dispense with Cantonese interpreters, the selection and training of personnel to run and staff the various courses, or the use which the Air Ministry ultimately envisaged making of officer cadets sent to complete their National Service at SOAS. On the other hand, preserved in the archives in full detail is an itemised list of the equipment which was to accompany No. 2 Course and its instructors on their journey from Wythall to Worth Matravers, including two cupboards, two steel filing cabinets and a typewriter, together with two electric and six portable gramophones 'complete with records', and seven items mysteriously labelled 'S.R. and R.U. Type 7'. Possibly these last-named were the ubiquitous Grundig reel-to-reel tape recorders remembered – if not always fondly – by all who experienced the mental rigours of RAF Chinese language training.[25]

No. 2 Course's stay at Worth Matravers lasted only a few months, since it was able to return to Wythall in October 1956 to occupy the billets and classrooms recently vacated by No. 1 Course. Members of No. 3 Course, which commenced at Worth Matravers in the autumn of 1956, were allowed to experience the delights of life on the picturesque Dorset coast for only slightly longer, for the Chinese language programme had now been assigned yet another home base: RAF Pucklechurch near Bristol. Like Wythall, this station had been established at the beginning of World War II as an operational centre for the barrage balloons which were intended to protect the nearby industrial city of Bristol from enemy bombing. At various times during the first decade after the war it housed Air Force Maintenance Units, the RAFVR, and a Ground Radio Servicing Squadron. When JSSL was consolidated at Tangmere in 1959 active operations ceased at Pucklechurch, and the eventual fate of at least part of the station was to become a remand centre and later a youth prison (Ashfield), for those subjected to a different kind of official detention.[26]

About No. 3 Course's move to Pucklechurch in April 1957 the archives are less informative than on the earlier move. Publicly accessible records tell us only the names of the students and instructors who in April 1957 travelled there by train from Worth Matravers, and what paraphernalia accompanied them, if any, remains a state secret.[27] Fortunately we are better informed about more important matters such as the organisation and character of Chinese language training at Pucklechurch. John Wright continued as director of studies, and he and his team of instructors, drawing on the experience of the previous eighteen months, were able to refine their teaching methods and course content in order to equip their students better for the practical tasks that lay ahead of them in Hong Kong.[28]

Pucklechurch continued to serve as a language school until September 1959, and six Chinese courses (Nos. 3 to 8 inclusive) underwent part or all of their training there. Those students who moved to Pucklechurch from Worth Matravers were forced to revert to a more typical service way of life, one that was distinctly less relaxed and more regimented, with regular station parades,[29] but the proximity to the fleshpots of Bristol and good communication links for trips home at the weekend were generally appreciated. The number of students on each course fluctuated, reaching a peak of 44-45 in 1958[30] and then declining to its lowest point with the last course before the ending of National Service (No. 11), in post-Pucklechurch days, for which a mere 15 students were selected.[31] Whatever the reason may be for these variations in numbers, it was an operational requirement that new courses should be (and indeed were) started up at regular six-month intervals, since the average length of time spent by a National Serviceman in Hong Kong between the completion of his training and his return to Britain for demobilisation was scarcely greater than that.

At the end of World War II the RAF was left with many bases which had been hurriedly put into service at the height of the Battle of Britain, but were clearly surplus to post-war needs. Wythall had already been marked down for closure, and only a short time after the move to Pucklechurch, that station's name too was added to the list.[32] On 27 May 1959 came the official announcement that JSSL would have a new home at Tangmere, a few miles outside Chichester in west Sussex, with the deployment there to be completed by 7 October.[33]

It appears always to have been the intention of the three services to have all language students (Russian, Chinese and others) stationed at the same camp for their entire training (both the basic pure language course and the short technical component towards the end), so that JSSL might be seen as a physical as well as a conceptual unity. Initially such a policy could not be put into effect. Unlike their Chinese counterparts, the Russian linguists had had to divide their year of language study between two different locations, first mastering the fundamentals at the decrepit naval air base at Crail in eastern Scotland (HMS Bruce),[34] and then moving on to Wythall or (from 1957) to Pucklechurch for the final weeks of technical training. Now, for the first time in the relatively brief history of JSSL, it had become possible to house under a single roof, as it were, all of its constituent parts – Russian and Chinese linguists, those learning the basics of their assigned language and those attempting to master its technical vocabulary and other tricks of their future trade.

The RAF station at Tangmere had had a longer history than either Wythall or Pucklechurch, and it held a much more glorious place on the wartime role of honour. The airfield was built at the end of World War I, and during World War II Tangmere served at different times as the home base for many of the Spitfire and Hurricane squadrons of Fighter Command. Later in the war it was used as the centre for Special Operations Executive (SOE) missions to get agents into and out of occupied France, and to recover aircrew downed in enemy-held territory. Some echoes of this storied past lingered even during the time of JSSL's residence there, for unlike Wythall and Pucklechurch it remained an operational air base, one which had earlier seen the breaking of world air speed records by Group Captain Teddy Donaldson's Gloster Meteor and Squadron Leader Neville Duke's Hawker Hunter, and which was still being used by Canberra bombers and Vickers Varsity training planes of Signals Command.[35] There was less reason, therefore, for those who studied Chinese at Tangmere to share the complaints of some of their predecessors who had felt cut off in their classrooms from the real work of the RAF to which they nominally belonged. An advance party of the 'RAF element of JSSL', which may have included members of No. 8 Chinese Course, arrived at Tangmere in August 1959,[36] and by mid-September the move from Pucklechurch had been completed.[37]

But by this time the end of National Service was already in sight, and even though some in the upper echelons of the Air Ministry expressed the view that 'full civilianisation [is] not practicable',[38] that was the reality for which both the service chiefs and their civilian counterparts at GCHQ now had to prepare. In 1960, less than a year after JSSL's move to Tangmere, it welcomed its last services Chinese course, for which a mere fifteen students had been selected: two regular soldiers and one regular airman, with the rest drawn from the RAF's final intake of National Servicemen.[39] By August, sensing that its role in language training was coming to an end, the Air Ministry had concluded that 'officer instructors at JSLS [JSSL] would not be replaced',[40] but in the event that conclusion turned out to be somewhat premature. Even though later courses were made up entirely of civilian students, we still hear of RAF instructors being posted to Tangmere and its successor station from 1964, North Luffenham in Rutland, to serve as Chinese language instructors.[41] It may not be too fanciful to interpret this as a tribute to the expertise in teaching languages for specific operational purposes which the RAF had built up from 1955 onwards; there was no need for GCHQ to try to replicate that expertise, virtually overnight, a task for which it was arguably ill suited.[42]

Notes

1   See Keegan (2003) *passim.*

2   Later Professor of Chinese at the Australian National University, and from 1965 onwards at Stockholm University; elected to the Swedish Academy in 1985.

3   Later a Professor of Chinese at Stanford University.

4   Later Professor of Chinese at Edinburgh University.

5   Later Professor of Chinese Literature at Harvard University.

6   Later Professor at the Chinese University of Hong Kong.

7   Mrs. Liu passed away in the spring of 2008, at the age of 93.

8   Names provided by Mick Rice, John Packer, John Hampson, Don Rimmington and other RAF linguists who studied at SOAS between 1951 and 1957.

9   Ken Sly remained in charge of Chinese language training until 1965, although with the ending of National Service in 1961 only civilian students (employees of GCHQ) took the courses offered thereafter.

10 An Air Ministry minute of 29 October 1953 (Minute 63, A. 145146/52) notes that the training in Cantonese of what were then termed 'Radio Telephony Direction Finder' operators (RTDF/Ops., the original cover trade description for linguists working in the field), was to be discontinued; AIR 2/11394 (RAF Personnel: Regular and National Service Entrants Selected for Training in Foreign Languages; Arrangements for Selection, Training and Conditions of Service, October 1952 to August 1955).

11 Paddy Raine kindly supplied much of the information contained in this paragraph.

12 Information from John Packer and others.

13 Based on information from John Hampson, David Raderecht and Don Rimmington.

14 Air Ministry Draft Order, 21 October 1952, AIR 2/11394. During the summer of 1953 airmen on the SOAS course were moved from Uxbridge to RAF West Ruislip and spent a few weeks there before proceeding to Wythall for technical training. This move possibly took place so that accommodation could be freed up at Uxbridge for some of the extra servicemen brought into the London area for special duty during Queen Elizabeth II's coronation.

15 Air Ministry Minute 65, 14 November 1953, AIR 2/11934: also see AIR 28/1410 (Pucklechurch Operations Records Book, January 1956 to December 1959).

16 AIR 28/1291 (Wythall Operations Record Book, May 1951 to December 1955). For further historical background on RAF Wythall see *www.wythallchurch.net/history/wasmc_raf_wythall. htm.*

17 Elliott/Shukman (2003), p. 172. The experience of working as a Russian linguist in Berlin, almost literally a stone's throw from the border fence, is amusingly described in Woodhead (2005).

18 A second possibility, that of having at least some of the language training carried out in the East, was considered by the Air Ministry at this time and apparently rejected: Minutes of Air Ministry meeting, 16 October 1953 (A.109893/51), AIR 2/11394.

19 Minutes of Air Ministry meeting, 10 July 1956, AIR 2/11935 (RAF Personnel: Regular and National Service Entrants Selected for Training in Foreign Languages; Arrangements for Selection, Training and Conditions of Service, August 1955 to January 1961).

20 AIR 28/1291.

21 AIR 28/1448 (Wythall Operations Record Book, January 1956 to December 1959).

22 Wythall Station Administrative Instruction No. 3/56, 18 June 1956, AIR 28/1448, and information from Keith Drury and others. Woodhead (2005), p. 77, has a tantalising reference to a 'hollow-eyed Navy man' allegedly studying Chinese at Pucklechurch in 1957, but to the best of the present authors' knowledge none of the 11 Chinese courses run by the RAF included naval personnel.

23 AIR 28/1448.

24 Information about the radar towers from John Norrish. For more on Watson-Watt's experiments see *www.purbeckradar.org.uk*.

25 Wythall Station Administrative Instruction No. 3/56, 18 June 1956, AIR 28/1448.

26 See *www.fishponds.free.com/puckle.htm* for a brief and occasionally inaccurate chronology of RAF Pucklechurch compiled by John Penny. Stephen Fry, the author and entertainer, spent three months as a 'guest' at Pucklechurch after its metamorphosis into a penal establishment for wayward youth: *en.wikipedia.org/wiki/Stephen_Fry*.

27 Appendix 'B' to RAF Wythall Admin. Instruction No. 1/57, in AIR 28/1448, officially records the date of the move to Pucklechurch as 6 April 1957, but according to diary notes of Mike Grindley, a member of No. 3 Course, the move in fact took place on 24 April. Mike thinks that this delay came about because the construction of living and studying quarters had fallen behind schedule, and in the event, classes for the new term for both No. 3 and No. 4 Course did not start until 30 April 1957.

28 Chapter 7 discusses course content and methodology in greater detail.

29 However several who like Mike Wallace arrived there later on, directly from their squarebashing experience, saw things in a different light; he found the discipline at Pucklechurch 'comparatively lax'.

30 Information from David Iliff.

31 Information from Keith Drury and Ken May.

32 Article in Bristol Evening Post, 28 October 1958, which stated that 'the decision was taken about 18 months ago by RAF No. 90 Signals Group'. It may be thought curious that the decision was first noted in the Pucklechurch Operations Record Book (AIR 28/1410) by clipping and pasting in this article, and not by reference to some internal administrative order issued and received during the preceding year and a half.

33 RAF Pucklechurch Administrative Order No. 1/59, 27 May 1959, AIR 28/1410.

34 Well described by Woodhead (2005).

35 Information about the history of RAF Tangmere drawn from *www.rafcaa.org.uk/admin/tangmere.htm* and *www.tangmere-museum.org.uk/history.htm*.

36 AIR 28/1426 (Tangmere Operations Record Book, January 1956 to December 1960).

37 AIR 28/1410.

38 Minutes of Air Ministry meeting, 9 December 1959, AIR 2/11395.

39 Information from Ken May.

40 Minutes of Language Training Planning Committee, 30 August 1960; M.2/S.2312, AIR 2/13255 (RAF Personnel: Language Training Requirements, Minutes). By this time JSSL was usually referred to as JSLS (Joint Services Language School).

41 AIR 28/1686 (Tangmere Operations Record Book, January 1961 to December 1965). Both RAF officers and native Chinese and Russian civilian instructors appear in a semi-official photograph taken at North Luffenham at 1969, and kindly made available to the authors by John Partridge.

42 Courses conducted by or on behalf of GCHQ from 1961 onwards are outside the scope of this work, but are referred to from time to time in Air Ministry records; see AIR 28/1686 and AIR 28/1628 (North Luffenham Operations Record Book, January 1961 to December 1966).

.

5

NEVER DARING TO ASK

'Laozi said: The wise man always keeps them innocent of knowledge, and ensures that the clever never dare to ask'
(Daodejing, 1.9)

Despite all the high level meetings and backroom planning, most young men were ill informed about the possibility of learning a language in the Forces. In the early 1950s there was of course no internet and minimal access to television, so that information about the Armed Services was limited to what was available from Recruiting Offices. With the exception of those in special circumstances, all young men expected to be conscripted, but most were skeptical about the potential benefits of two years' service unless a trade that would be useful in later life was offered. Thus there were trade options such as motor mechanic or electrical engineer that were popular requests from men hoping to make use of training opportunities during their two years, but the Services trained only as many as were needed, and did not see themselves as managers of a national training scheme. Similarly, many who were accepted into the RAF – about a quarter of all conscripts – fancied becoming aircrew, but in late 1956 the RAF stopped recruiting National Servicemen for flying duties,[1] and in practice many National Servicemen in the RAF never saw the inside of an aircraft. In any case, training in a manual trade did not appeal to those with professional qualifications or aspirations. There was no public information such as one can now find on the RAF careers website.

To many who became Chinese linguists, the means of arriving in that trade were mysterious and something of a lottery. It was never very clear to the young men who were called to their first medical examination and an initial interview at the local Ministry of Labour offices, what value if any was placed on the choice of service that they requested. There was an assumption that the RAF took the better educated, but however many requested the RAF – and possibly no records of individual requests were ever kept – only one out of every four National Servicemen were accepted into this branch of the Forces.

After 1953 all RAF recruits went to the reception camp at Cardington near Bedford.[2] About twice a month a few hundred young men arrived there, to be kitted out and to learn the rudiments of the systems that were to rule their lives for the next two years. Whilst many were anxious about the progress of their lives in the forces, in which their activities for the next two years were yet to be decided, the transfer from the reception centre to basic training camp was as daunting as the first rail journey, often made alone, to Cardington. Mike Wallace, who was on No. 7 Course, movingly records

> I had the feeling of joining a vast organisation, and in the 1950s it was. Our armed forces were still at considerable strength and Britain's commitment stretched all over the globe. There seemed to be hundreds of us as we boarded the special train that waited for us in the branch line dedicated to RAF Cardington. As we steamed our way to RAF Bridgnorth for 'square bashing' the singing began and brought home to me the various British 'tribes' represented. The Scots sang tartan songs, the Welsh gave us memories of the valleys and I'm afraid we English could only respond with popular songs of the day like 'My old man's a dustman'.

Other British 'tribes' not represented were the Northern Irish (who were not conscripted, to avoid stirring political unrest) and – though there was no formal policy about this – very few of the increasing black population.

Part of this induction included instruction about and aptitude tests for the various trades which were available in the RAF, this information being repeated in greater detail at subsequent Basic Training.. The amount of information available to assist in making a request for a particular trade was inconsistent. Most of those who became linguists had somehow heard through the grapevine that courses in a foreign language were available, but had little further information. The next hurdle was the language aptitude test, but in order to take this one had first to be aware that language training in the Armed Forces was possible, and this information was not always obvious to raw recruits. Thus, in spite of the cynical ethos of never volunteering for anything, applicants for language courses were almost all self-selected, though how they found their way into this esoteric activity varied.

One of the authors of this book recorded that on the third day at Cardington an officer giving a lecture about available trades told him that there was not much chance of an educational training course in a language unless the end of one's basic training happened to coincide with the start of a course. Later on at the Basic Training camp at Hednesford, an officer dealing with trade training was more encouraging, and mentioned Russian and Chinese, with the training taking place in Bodmin – being so little travelled, even in Britain, the idea of spending a year in Cornwall appealed to this raw recruit, whatever the activity there (this idyllic vision was not shared by the Russian linguists who were sent there!).[3]

Others had different motives. Mike Wallace writes that

> The choices were between on the one hand Russian and the Soviet bloc countries and on the other hand Chinese. I'm ashamed to say that my decision was based on the fact that the Russian [course] was up in Scotland while Chinese was at RAF Pucklechurch near Bristol. As I was very serious about a Cheltenham girl (whom I later married) it was no contest!

The means of getting onto a course were also not clear. Evidently a National Serviceman could not apply for officer training and at the same time for linguist training leading to a posting abroad, but in other ways the RAF's policy seems to have been quite pragmatic – on at least one course a small number of conscripts had signed on as regulars because they had understood that was the only way to get on a language course, and although they soon found out that the majority of trainees were not regulars, they were not allowed to withdraw their signing-on papers. Perhaps at some points during the years of National Service, Education Officers were encouraged to publicise the opportunity for language training; at other times in other places, it seemed that basic information was restricted. An Education Officer told John Norrish (No. 3 Course) that he would be learning colloquial Chinese, giving the impression that the job would somehow involve interviewing civilians (this may relate to the re-naming of categories of linguists as described in chapter 3).

Another informant – one of the relatively few who studied Chinese as a National Serviceman before the internal courses began – recalls how, after starting RAF training as an Air Traffic Controller, he happened to see an advertisement on the station notice-board for a Chinese language course at the School of Oriental and African Studies (SOAS, London University). Although the closing date for applications was past, he wrote in, was summoned for interview and accepted for inclusion on the course. He had to take a hearing test, designed to decide to which of two courses a trainee should be assigned – Mandarin with its four vocal tones or Cantonese with its more complex system of tones. It appears that at this time – the beginning of the academic year 1952-53 – it was still the RAF's intention to train linguists in both Mandarin and Cantonese, and several airmen, including John Packer, took the Cantonese course; but at some point during the academic year either the Air Ministry itself, or one of the various bodies with an interest in Chinese communications intelligence, decided that there was now an operational requirement for Mandarin alone. So when the year ended John and his Cantonese-speaking colleagues were offered the choice of staying on at SOAS for a further year to study Mandarin, or redeployment elsewhere in the RAF, while those who had studied

Mandarin went out to Hong Kong to undertake intercept duties.

The choice of language was not normally open to the applicant. Among those recruits who had an academic bent, it became fairly common knowledge that some National Servicemen learnt Russian, so the majority of those who volunteered for language training assumed that they would be offered that language, and it came as a considerable surprise to be told that the only vacancies were in Chinese.. As John Henty (No. 6 Course) records:

> About halfway into the eight week [basic training] course, I was called in with others to take a language aptitude test for Chinese, of all things. This was not what I had in mind. We were presented by Sqn Ldr Wright with pages of hieroglyphics to copy and strange sounds to listen to. Was it my imagination or did the Squadron Leader have slanted eyes and a drooping moustache? I seemed to satisfy him as soon after I was given two weeks leave and a rail warrant to some place named Pucklechurch near Bristol, which even the clerk issuing the warrant hadn't heard of. So I left Wilmslow with my first claim to fame, never having passed out from basic training.

After previous employment as a travel agent, Keith Drury (No. 11 Course) was set down for training as a teleprinter operator, but his brother, who had left the RAF several years previously, though not a linguist, had suggested to Keith that he should ask about language training. The trades selection officer had little information, but undertook to find out more, and a few days later Keith found himself on the way to Tangmere, having completed only three weeks of 'square bashing'.

This was not however a unique experience, as men selected for language training were sometimes relieved from basic training very early in their service, whilst others who were accepted on the courses had to wait in other mundane occupations for three or four months. Both Keith Scott (of No. 1 Course) and Peter Treacher

(No. 3 Course) spent some time as clerical assistants at Yatesbury, a large radio training establishment in the Wiltshire Downs. But a member of No. 6 Course, Mike Prada, completed only two weeks of basic training at Wilmslow because of a hospital admission with pneumonia, and on discharge went straight on the course, never having fired a gun. However, on arrival at Pucklechurch this raw recruit found himself taking part in 'months of drill rehearsals' for Remembrance Day in Bristol. 'The Remembrance Day parade eventually took place', he recollects, 'in pouring rain, which made the change of webbing from white to blue leaving my greatcoat streaked with blanco.' Yet another would-be linguist, Ken Brooks of No. 8 Course, completed only five and a half weeks of square bashing before being re-routed to the language school. The decision to apply for the language aptitude test seems to have been largely that of the applicant – and it is not known how many servicemen applied and were turned down following the test – but getting on one of the courses depended partly on the coincidence of call-up date and course starting date.

Another man designated to become trainee teleprinter operator was Bill Mellows of No. 4 Course. At the end of his basic training at West Kirby, he was excused the passing-out parade because of a twisted ankle, and was due seven days' leave with a travel warrant to return to RAF Compton Bassett; but a message came to say that this posting was cancelled, and he was instead to report to Pucklechurch as an 'A & S Asst. Ling (C)'.[4]

To some extent the possession of a basic language qualification naturally helped the application. Ken May, also of No. 11 Course, wrote:

> My greatest fear was that with NS slowly coming to an end, I would find myself in a meaningless job simply passing the time somewhere inconvenient for two years. When I saw the trade 'linguist' on a notice board, I did not have a clue what it would entail, and there did not seem to be much additional information available.

However, he did already have two G.C.E. 'O' levels in European languages and was accepted, but had to wait working in a sports kit loan store until the next course became available. Another suggestion to explain the procedures, advanced by Don Rimmington who was selected for SOAS training in 1955 as an officer cadet, was that Classics-trained students were relatively well placed when faced with Chinese because they did not expect to make direct transfers from one language to another:

> When learning Chinese [you] had to lay aside most of your previous European-based language learning experience. Of the 15 of us who went to SOAS [in 1955] , I think that three or four had done Classics, though it has to be said that the others came from a range of backgrounds – history, modern languages, art history, architecture, accountancy, etc.

It seems that only a very few initially and deliberately applied for the Mandarin programme. One of those who did was Donald Sutton (No. 5 Course) who before call-up had heard about Russian courses but when he asked about them at square bashing he was told they were filled up. Nevertheless he was offered the choice of two other languages of which one was Chinese, and his choice was partly influenced by a friend of his father's, the sinologist Otto van der Sprenkel, who had given him a book on Chinese while he was still at school.

Although no factual confirmation can be found in available records, it seems likely that these apparently rather haphazard selection procedures, like the numbers of students on each course, were dictated by the services' attempts to respond to the ever-changing requirements of the Cold War. As always, the higher command had to plan for the perceived development or remission of threats at least a year ahead; and on a scale as small as that of Chinese-speaking linguists, the calculation also had to include the number and availability of regular personnel. Towards the end of the 1950s, when it was clear that civilianisation of some part of the foreign language sector was inevitable, the numbers of conscripts required were naturally reduced. But these intricacies of management planning were not evident to language-training recruits, who felt themselves simultaneously marginalised in a backwater of the RAF, having 'failed' to obtain their first choice of training in Russian, and yet specially chosen for a job which was offered to only a tiny number of conscripted men.

The aptitude tests themselves were by and large seen as entertaining rather than threatening examinations (at least by those who passed). Usually a brief aural test – to check that one could hear the tonal inflections that are an integral part of Mandarin – was followed by a written test based on a mock Esperanto language (or, as one contributor declares, an Afghan language!). Provided with a small vocabulary and limited rules of grammar of this invented language, the applicants were given a very short time to learn these and then invited to translate from and into English without further reference to the given information. Within a few weeks – sometimes within days – the selected students found themselves spending seven hours a day immersed in learning, from scratch, another totally new but now real language.

Notes

1   Hickman (2004), chapter 4.

2   Prior to 1953 the RAF's reception centre was at Padgate near Warrington. Cardington was famed as the original home of gas balloon dirigibles, culminating in the ill-fated R101, hence its enormous hangars which are still preserved today.

3   Elliott/Shukman (2003), chapter 6 *passim*.

4   'Accounting & Secretarial Assistant, Linguist (Chinese)'.

6

GWOYEU ROMATZYH
('NATIONAL ROMANISATION')[1]

'The Chinese government has given this question of Romanized spelling some consideration ... but the system evolved by the government is still in a more or less tentative form and has not come into general use.'
(R.H. Mathews, Preface to the first edition of A Chinese-English Dictionary, 1931)

Europeans had been in contact with China for many centuries, but their presence in China was either forbidden or restricted by Imperial Edict. The early Portuguese traders were granted a tiny enclave in Macao in the mid-sixteenth Century,[2] and over time they were followed by numbers of other western European traders. This slow build-up of foreign pressure eventually led to armed conflict between China and Britain which resulted in Hong Kong Island being ceded to the UK in 1842.[3] One famous Jesuit scholar, Matteo Ricci (1552-1610),[4] spent nearly twenty years in China, first in Macao and then in Guangdong province, before travelling further around the northern part of the country, and finally being permitted to present himself at the Court of the Wan-Li Emperor in Beijing in 1601.

However it was not until the Treaty of Nanking was concluded between China and Britain in 1842 that the way was opened for foreign traders and missionaries to be permitted to live in a selected number of China's coastal cities. So western missionaries and scholars set about learning the Chinese language, and to make this task easier they used a form of romanisation based on the Latin letters of the western European alphabet to represent Chinese sounds. From this base they could learn the spoken language, and then if they so wanted they could undertake the demanding task of learning the written language and become proficient in translating their religious tracts in order to propagate the Christian faith. This was the main factor motivating their actions, as they needed to acquire knowledge of the Chinese language and culture in order to be successful in converting the Chinese; to be fair to them it also became a two-way process because they gradually started translating Classical Chinese books into European languages as well, including the works of Confucius and Mencius. At that time most written Chinese was in the classical form, using characters which, for the mass of illiterate Chinese who were unable to read any public notices or edicts, represented the might and authority of the Emperor. Only a small cohort of top men appointed by the Emperor, made up of educated officials and bureaucrats, could read Classical Chinese, and for these power-holders the written language was a significant instrument for controlling the population and maintaining this autocratic form of government, as well as their own favourable niches in society. And the Imperial system of rule in China was not overthrown until 1911.

There had been different systems of Latinised writing used to represent Chinese language sounds in western countries and these spellings varied according to the phonetic parameters of each particular mother tongue involved, that is, English, French, German and so on. In the English-speaking world the early popular form of romanisation was Wade-Giles, a system developed by two British diplomat-scholars of the Victorian era.[5] R.H. Mathews produced his monumental *Chinese-English Dictionary* using a form of Wade-Giles, and this book has proved to be a valuable tool for western scholars in the Chinese field; so much so that Harvard University Press issued a Revised American Edition in 1943 with corrections, revisions and extra entries plus an additional section on 'Introduction on Pronunciation', and by 1956 it was into its seventh printing.

The 1943 edition had 1226 pages, containing 7763 characters with appropriate romanisation attached to each one to indicate the sound and tone in the norther Chinese language, and there were copious lists of all the related compound words for each character. And this dictionary is still on sale today. It should be remembered that western scholars of Chinese were each building on the original researches done by their predecessors in the nineteenth century, and Mathews in the preface to his dictionary did acknowledge his indebtedness to Baller's Analytical Chinese-English Dictionary, by then out of print and, as Mathews put it, 'now out of date'. To put matters in perspective, before World War II the Chinese field in the UK was a rare academic subject for ordinary undergraduates, and the language was studied mainly to satisfy the requirements of the Foreign & Colonial Office, the military, various missionary groups, businessmen, commercial traders and the occasional academic or eccentric.

The origins of the G.R. (Gwoyeu Romatzyh)[6] system of romanisation lay within the stormy history of the early stages of China's modernisation in the 1920s. In 1921 when Bertrand Russell[7] was in China on a teaching and lecture tour his Chinese secretary was a young scholar called Chao Yuanren.[8] What effect Russell had on him is not known, but several years later Chao was working to develop a romanisation system for the (northern) Chinese language along with Lin Yutang and others, and in conjunction with the 'Preparatory Commission for the Unification of the National Language' during 1925-26. This system was publicly unveiled on 26 September 1928, and the main credit for its development is ascribed to Chao Yuanren. To what extent it was implemented in China's educational system and how much it was used in printed textbooks is difficult to say, for in those days children in Chinese schools were able to learn the pronunciation of characters using the 'bo-po-mo-fo' system[9] This

58

was an old phonetic system for transcribing Mandarin, created in China in the early twentieth century using an alphabet of thirty-seven special symbols based on Chinese calligraphy; it is still in use in Taiwan today. So Chinese school teachers would have had to choose between this home-grown Chinese phonetic system or the foreign romanised script, that is to say G.R.. Of the two options, the Chinese phonetic system would be much easier for the teachers to cope with than Gwoyeu Romatzyh. It was noted by Mathews in the 1931 preface to his *Chinese-English Dictionary*:

> The Chinese government has given the question of Romanized spelling some consideration, and a society to investigate the matter has recently been formed, but the system evolved by the government is still in a more or less tentative form and has not come into general use. The object of that system is to give, as far as possible, a rendering in Roman letters which will obviate the use of figures or other marks to indicate the different tones, so that a reader would be able to give a fairly accurate rendering of the Chinese sounds without a knowledge of the characters.

One product arising from these endeavours was the publication in 1932 in Shanghai of an official pronunciation dictionary[10] which used the G.R. system, and which was called the 'Gwoin Charngyonq Tzyhhuey' (National Pronunciation General Usage Dictionary). From the vantage point of hindsight G.R. did not apparently flourish in its country of origin for any significant length of time, but it was later promoted in Britain in the 1940s by Professor Walter Simon, who enlisted the assistance of Dr. C.H. Lu in producing textbooks for learning Chinese. Both of these men were based at the School of Oriental and African Studies (SOAS) in London University, and together they published textbooks combining Chinese characters, G.R. and English, to be used in the teaching of Mandarin Chinese. To go with these course textbooks, Professor Simon also produced his Chinese-English Dictionary, published in 1947, using G.R. as the romanised medium to indicate the syllabic sound and tone of each Chinese character. In his preface he paid tribute to Professor Y R Chao as follows:

It is befitting that the first Chinese-English Dictionary based on Gwoyeu Romatzyh should be dedicated to the Chinese scholar who is primarily responsible for this system. The publishers and I are greatly obliged to Professor Y.R. Chao (Jaw Yuan Renn) for having accepted the dedication. May this dictionary win new friends for the Chinese language and in this way for China itself. (Walter Simon, Twickenham, London, 5 January 1946)

All compilers of Chinese dictionaries should be applauded, but on examining his dictionary today after a long period of time, one can only praise Professor Simon for the scholarly care that he gave to this work; it was a veritable labour of love.[11] Likewise the Mathews dictionary evokes a similar response.

To explain G.R. in simple terms, the Roman alphabet spelling for every Chinese syllable indicated both the phonetic sound and which of the four tones of Mandarin was required for it. So anyone who could read G.R. would know the Chinese sound and tone of a syllable immediately. Here are some examples of the four tones written in G.R.:

1st Tone (Level)	2nd Tone (Rising)	3rd Tone (Falling/rising)	4th Tone (Falling)
chiu	*chyu*	*cheu*	*chiuh*
mha	*ma*	*maa*	*mah*
iou	*you*	*yeou*	*yow*
lhiang	*liang*	*leang*	*lianq*
tzy	*tzyr*	*tzyy*	*tzyh*

Yet although G.R. was produced by enlightened Chinese scholars working within China it did not seem to catch on. The traditional Chinese psyche may have contained a distrust of things foreign such as the Roman alphabet letters, but a major inhibiting factor was the instability prevailing in the 1920s and 1930s which created chaotic social, political and economic conditions and permitted the gradual Japanese military occupation of the North East and key coastal provinces, leading up to the start of the Sino-Japanese War in 1937.

It was not until after the unification of China in 1949 that a standard system of romanisation was introduced in the 1950s by the newly established Government of the Chinese People's Republic. This system was called Hanyu Pinyin ('Chinese Language Spelling'), and it used diacritical marks above the romanisation of each syllable to denote the tone used in the National Language. This technique was borrowed from the Yale University system.[12] Yale romanisation had been adopted by the US authorities in World War II as a more accurate representation of Chinese phonetic sounds than Wade-Giles, and it thus provided their military personnel with a faster and more effective means of learning Mandarin. However, when looking at the whole table of Hanyu Pinyin spellings they seem to be an eclectic mix taken from the key romanisation systems, and there are some innovations too, such as the introduction of the letters c, q, x, z and zh to represent initial consonant sounds.

For speakers of English the three main systems of romanisation were Wade-Giles, G.R. and Yale, and they were in general usage up to the 1950s and 1960s, before the Hanyu Pinyin system created by the People's Republic of China gradually became paramount. As an illustration of this point Don Rimmington, an officer cadet on No. 1 Course and later Professor of Chinese at Leeds University, remembers that in the UK university field in the 1950s, Oxford, Cambridge and Durham were using Wade-Giles while SOAS used G.R., and he recalls that when Leeds established its Chinese programme in 1963 it started off with Yale romanisation but soon converted to Pinyin, using textbooks published in Beijing for teaching purposes. It actually took some time before Pinyin became the accepted romanisation system for university teaching in Britain. The following comparative table of examples of the main forms of romanisation gives some idea of the differing spellings for the same Chinese syllabic sound.

Hanyu Pinyin	G.R.	Wade-Giles	Yale
biáo	byau	piao^2	býau
cōng	tsong	ts'ung^1	tsūng
xué	shyue	hsueh^2	sýwe
zhōng	jong	chung^1	jūng
zuō	tzuo	tso^1	dzwō

As a further example here is a simple English sentence transcribed into the four different romanisation systems:

English Sentence   I don't want to go to China.
Gwoyeu Romatzyh (G.R.) Woo bwu yaw daw Jonggwo chiuh.
Hanyu Pinyin: Wǒ bú yaò daò Zhōngguó qù.
Yale: Wǒ bú yàu dàu Jūnggwó chỳu.
Wade-Giles   Wo^3 pu^2 yao^4 tao^4 Chung^{1}kuo^2 ch'ü^4.

Whatever the strong or weak points of Wade-Giles, Yale, G.R. and other romanised forms, the Hanyu Pinyin system has finally superceded them all, and while it has become the standard form of Chinese romanisation used globally today, the old systems can still be found surviving in battered copies of old textbooks and dictionaries in university libraries, secondhand bookshops and attics throughout the world, and on websites too. However it would be unwise to write off those old forms too quickly, because Blackwell's Bookshop in Oxford currently[13] has brand new copies of the R.H. Mathews dictionary on the shelves (exactly the same as the 1943 revised American edition, but there is no date of publication given), and Yale romanisation still has its uses in the teaching of Cantonese and Korean.[14] Needless to say G.R. is indelibly imprinted in the hearts and minds of all the Chinese linguists on the eleven RAF National Service courses from 1955-61 and of the small number of regular servicemen who were also involved. Amen!

Notes

1 Gwoyeu Romatzyh (G.R.): in its early days G.R. was sometimes translated as 'National Romanisation' when it should in fact have been 'National Language Romanisation.'

2 *whc.unesco.org/en/list/1110.*

3 Twitchett/Fairbank (1978).

4 *www.britannica.com/eb/article-9063525/Matteo-Ricci.*

5 *www.britannica.com/eb/article-9075831/Wade-Giles-romanization.*

6 'Gwoyeu Romatzyh' should strictly be written as 'Gwoyeu Luomaatzyh' because the transliteration of the city of Rome into Chinese is 'Luomaa'.

7 See Russell (1968), Part III – China.

8 *en.wikipedia.org/wiki/Yuan_Ren_Chao.*

9 *en.wikipedia.org/wiki/Zhuyin.*

10 See 'Introduction on Pronunciation' in Mathews (1943).

11 Simon (1947).

12 *en.wikipedia.org/wiki/Pinyin* and *en.wikipedia.org/wiki/Yale_Romanization#Mandarin.*

13 As of Reginald Hunt's visit in July 2007.

14 *en.wikipedia.org/wiki/Yale_Romanization#Korean* and *en.wikipedia.org/wiki/Yale_Romanization#Cantonese.*

7

LEARNING AND REPEATING

'The Master [Confucius] said: Is it not a pleasure
to learn something and then repeat it at the right time?'
(Confucian Analects 1.1)

Education Officers responsible for administering the language
aptitude tests for the language training courses were naturally very
cautious about giving their views on which school subjects would
best serve the candidates in the study of Chinese. Their studied
non-committal approach engendered the feeling that being good at
science or music could be just as valuable as being good at European
languages or Classics. Most ex-linguists remember being presented
with some basic words and simple sentences in an artificial language,
and they were either given language rules or they had to identify
any language rules, followed by some translation work both ways
and recognition exercises of Chinese sounds. John Norrish (No. 3
Course) reflects on the aptitude testing he and others from his course
underwent before being selected to start on their training:

> As I recall it, those few airmen who were volunteering for the
> No. 3 Chinese Course were taken from Wilmslow to Hednesford
> to meet volunteers from other basic training camps for the
> aptitude test. With hindsight, what we experienced must have
> been a pre-publication version of the well known Modern
> Languages Aptitude Test (Carroll & Sapon, 1958), because the
> sections in this test battery show all the components that we
> were tested on. It went as follows:

1. We were shown samples of a language and were asked to work out 'the grammar rules' from them and then construct sentences from them.
2. We were asked to pick out and memorise new sounds to test phonetic acuity.
3. As for vocabulary, we had to work out how the words functioned in sentences; this also related to grammar.
4. Words and 'rules' were committed to memory and translations were made to and from the language.
   One of the theoretical problems with this set of tests is that it relies on the view that language learning is entirely conscious; later research (e.g. Stephen Krashen and many others) indicates strongly that this is not necessarily the case, that what is 'acquired' unconsciously rather than deliberately 'learnt', is more likely to be internalised. However, in this case, given the overpowering motivation to remain on the course and not be 'returned to unit' (RTU), the process proved rather successful in its predictions as I recall very few of our number enduring this fate.

Nevertheless the volunteer linguists went through the tests and those that satisfied the various challenges posed by these linguistic exercises were temporarily posted around RAF stations in the UK, some in Pool Flights, awaiting the start of their Chinese course. A few trainees, through the serendipity of RAF needs and the timing of their service entry which happened to be just before the start of the next Chinese course, were able to avoid some or all of the square bashing experience.

Yet in spite of the cumbersome bureaucracy of such a large service organisation, 39 selected recruits were summoned to assemble at RAF Wythall, near Birmingham, sometime in late September 1955 for the No. 1 Chinese Training Course. Sqn Ldr J.D. Wright and Flight Lieutenant (Flt Lt) J.A. Cant had been posted to Wythall on 5 September 1955 to set things up,[1] and they both figured prominently in the early success of this experimental programme, and deserve a lot of credit for the achievement of producing Chinese linguists to satisfy the voice interception requirements of 367 Signals Unit, RAF Little Sai Wan, Hong Kong. The Reverend Paddy Raine, who was the Commanding Officer of RAF Batty's Belvedere from 1955 to 1957, made this recent assessment on the job effectiveness of the Chinese linguists in collecting intelligence data:

> To the extent that the trained linguists provided a lot of raw information to those who had the task of analysing it, I consider that the language training was successful.

Trainees on the early courses led by 'Squaddy' Wright and Joe Cant still speak warmly of them and regard them as the key figures in the early days of the RAF Chinese language teaching programme. At the beginning of No. 1 Course 'Squaddy' Wright, as officer in charge, gave the group one introductory lecture which was on the honorifics of addressing people, polite expressions and cultural points, but otherwise he rarely appeared in a teaching capacity. His time must have been fully occupied on the organisational and administrative side of things, as well as keeping an eye on the teaching materials needed in class each day. Nevertheless he was a constant presence in the background, overseeing everything and with his finger on the pulse. Ex-linguists all agree that he was well respected, and he made every effort to protect his charges from the attentions of any over-zealous officers or NCOs from outside the programme. Whilst being reasonably tolerant of youthful exuberance, when he was pushed too far various courses reported that he could deliver an appropriate bawling out that was always respectfully delivered. Mike Grindley recounts that No. 3 Course were especially appreciative of the quality of 'Squaddy' Wright's bollockings, but took very little notice of them.

Flt Lt Joe Cant was obviously in charge of the classroom side of things, and he and his team of native Chinese instructors and SOAS-trained NCOs took over the bulk of the timetable teaching of the trainees. He himself at a later stage became Officer-in-Charge of the Chinese language courses for a time in 1958, before being replaced by Sqn Ldr W.D. Blythe in January 1959. Meanwhile the trainees sat in their classrooms in the security compound for much of the working week (estimated at around 30-35 hours), and as they were conscripted members of Her Majesty's Armed Forces they faced the reality that they were captive students with an 100% attendance required from them for two years. On top of this they had to cope with the underlying pressure of studying hard in order to avoid being withdrawn from the course and re-mustered to another trade: in Air Force terminology RTU – Returned To Unit. The last factor may have helped their motivation and work ethic, but most of the trainees usually had an initial interest, or developed some interest, in learning this esoteric language, which was so different from any of their European linguistic experiences. To illustrate the general level of commitment of the trainees: there have been rare reports of dropouts from the eleven courses, while a few did fail the final examination and some of these were re-mustered.

Most trainees felt the security restraint to be quite a serious matter, and so on going home at weekends their families had to be content with the minimal information that their son was on an obscure Chinese language course of some kind, and that was it. This mental stricture imposed upon trainees to constantly remember the security blackout on their studies was a reality which faced all of them on their home leaves, although in all seriousness it could not have been too demanding for family and friends to put two and two together to work out likely jobs for them to do after such a course of training. It was rather reminiscent of the wartime slogan 'Careless talk costs lives' in a much lighter version, but nevertheless trainees had to be secretive about their work, even with family. Steve Fletcher (No. 1 Course) has a little vignette about this:

> When I was learning Mandarin at RAF Wythall in 1955 I used to have a 36 hour pass on most weekends and hitchhiked home to London. I was a pseudo-beatnik, and Saturday evenings found me either at a Jazz Club or one of the dances that were held at the Art Schools of central London. At one such dance at St Martin's School of Art I was in the company of a very attractive student of ceramics

who introduced me to two of her fellow-students both of whom were Chinese. I could not resist the temptation to display my knowledge of their native language and they were amazed to hear my conversation, although I did not reveal the source of my learning, much to their curiosity. One of the Chinese was Michael Chow who later became an actor in James Bond films, and subsequently opened Mr Chow's Restaurant in Knightsbridge. The other student, Henry Lee, when I mentioned that I was going to Hong Kong, asked me if I would take some of his art work to his brother who lived in Kowloon. I took the pictures to Hong Kong but never hurried to get in touch with his brother who he said worked at a bookshop in Nathan Road. When I eventually went to the bookshop, a sort of Hong Kong equivalent of Foyles, it transpired that his brother owned said massive bookshop and he was, to say the least, immensely rich with a huge mansion in the New Territories. He and his family entertained me and a friend several times and when my friend demonstrated his considerable musical skills Mr Lee hired him to teach his two young daughters to play piano. When I returned to the UK and was demobbed I heard that Michael Chow had married my student friend and Henry Lee had already returned to Hong Kong. I never saw him again.

All Chinese linguists had to tread this narrow line on security and no evidence has been revealed that any transgressed on this. One example of seemingly lax security is illustrated by an anecdote from Dave Haysom (later a Russian linguist) whose uncle's quarry by chance lay close to RAF Worth Matravers. On a visit there around 1956-57 he came across a group of Chinese linguist students strolling along the lanes near the camp, in civvies, in the company of a Chinese tutor, practising what he assumed to be the Chinese tones as they walked – quite a bizarre sight in a remote corner of rural England.

The RAF was constantly tested in various other ways too, a not uncommon challenge being the wish of a few regular airmen in Hong Kong to marry a Chinese woman. One or two of the regulars did indeed have Chinese wives, but common talk in the billets always brought up the names of NCOs who had been immediately flown back to the UK on putting in a request to get married. This was yet another minor cross-cultural issue for the linguists in Hong Kong to ponder, because the RAF policy appeared to be against marriage to a Chinese woman. David Iliff remembers that in the late 1950s two RAF Sergeant Technicians, both Chinese speakers, and each with a Chinese wife, were teaching instructors on the Chinese courses. Unfortunately, when security was tightened one wife did not get the required security clearance from the RAF and as a result her husband was re-mustered to another trade.

In the classroom the foundation stone for the initial teaching and learning of spoken Chinese were the main course books EM 506 and EM 507. The starter book EM 506[2] was a thick, foolscap, typewritten manual consisting of twelve Units spread over more than two hundred pages, with a complete glossary at the end, and all the Chinese vocabulary was written in Latin letters in a form of romanisation called Gwoyeu Romatzyh (G.R.: literally, 'National Language Roman Letters');[3] in fact there was not one single written Chinese character in the book. The final words of the 'Introduction' explicitly affirmed this teaching approach:

> No attempt should be made to learn or teach the written language until the first twelve units of this course have been thoroughly mastered.

The original U.S. War Department Education Manual 506[4] was entitled Spoken Chinese, a basic language course for absolute beginners which used the Yale form of romanisation. It was produced by the American Armed Forces, with the US authors and sources clearly stated, and the date of publication given as 2 January 1944. So it is a reasonable assumption that it had been used for teaching US personnel from the latter stages of World War II onwards. The introduction specified that it was for learners of the 'North Chinese' dialect, which dates it somewhat, as today that language would be more familiar to western readers when described as Modern Standard Chinese, Mandarin, National Language or Putonghua.

The follow-up manual EM507[5] was by the same two authors, and was published a year later on 2 January 1945. It adopted exactly the same style and structure as EM506, consisting of eighteen Units, numbered 13-30. Together these two books constituted a 'Basic Course in Spoken Chinese' totalling thirty Units of study spread over 617 pages. They introduced Chinese grammatical points step by step in a solid, systematic way, and every linguistic item was thoroughly clarified in detail and then consolidated by a range of related exercises and drills. EM507 had exactly the same learning philosophy as EM506 of not using written Chinese characters, except that right at the back of the book could be found a short theoretical outline on the Chinese writing system, and within this explanation eighteen Chinese characters were used. In the original US education manuals the Yale system of romanisation was used to represent the sounds and tones of the Chinese words, but the RAF had painstakingly transcribed the whole book from the Yale form into their preferred system of romanisation, which was G.R. These two manuals were reprinted in 1955 in G.R., with a note on the front stating that they were for the use of the RAF only, but although the system of romanisation had been changed, the books still retained the American reference codes EM506 and EM507. One of the sergeants teaching No. 1 Course claimed to have been the main transcriber of the G.R. romanisation used in EM 506, and this was enough to impress the trainees, giving him increased kudos within the group.

Classes were usually in small groups of 8 to 12 trainees, dependent on course numbers, and the initial teaching emphasis was on accurate pronunciation of Chinese syllables and getting the tones right; then there were basic structures, plus lots of listening and drilling of Chinese and simple conversation exercises. Mike Grindley noted in his diary on 30 April 1957 that the newly-arrived No. 4 Course had started their studies on that day at Pucklechurch and would suffer three weeks of intensive tone practice trying to reproduce Chinese syllabic sounds.

EM506 was an ideal teaching and learning book for Spoken Chinese, and the situational conversations in all of the 12 Units revolved around the life of Mr Ross, Mr Wang and Mr Hu, with cameo appearances by two American soldiers called Johnson and Ward. Basic everyday vocabulary and structures were introduced systematically and explained very fully and effectively, as well as any relevant historical facts or cultural practices. Judging by results, both manuals EM506 and 507 proved to be successful course books for learners of spoken Chinese because trainees were getting quite a balanced range of oral-aural work per day, so much so that even around fifty years later most ex-linguists can still say a few words in passable Chinese. Mike Wallace (No. 7 Course) used his knowledge of Chinese in a letter to the *Daily Mail* in 2007 to explain the origin of the English phrase 'long time no see'. He attributed it to the eighteenth century British traders on the China coast who translated it word for word from the Chinese saying 'hao jeou mei jiann' (G.R.). He recalled that as a student at the RAF languages school at Pucklechurch in the 1950s he offered 'I don't see any good wine' as a theoretically correct translation, because 'jeou' can mean either 'long time' or 'wine', and only seeing the Chinese characters would make the distinction clear.

The content and vocabulary of the teaching manuals were concerned with ordinary aspects of daily life, but after the groups had ploughed through them, the next stage of the language programme provided another US based course book of twenty lessons[6] which strongly focussed on military and flying terminology, and which was commonly known to trainees as 'Cloudy Bill' or 'Nebulous Neddy'. The first lesson was about the problems of an American flyer who parachuted into North East China, a situation very reminiscent of the Korean War, and all subsequent lessons revolved around American military personnel and related vocabulary. Other significant teaching material came from textbooks, all using Gwoyeu Romatzyh, that were written and compiled by Walter Simon and others, such as:

Chinese Reader and Guide to Conversation (Simon and C.H. Lu)

Chinese Sentence Series (Simon)

Structure Drill in Chinese (Simon and T.C. Chao).[7]

There was also a book compiled by Flt Lt Clifford Phillips, *English-Chinese Handbook of Royal Air Force Terminology.*[8]

Later stages of the course became more closely related to operational needs and involved much listening material consisting of four-figure blocs of Chinese numbers, which trainees had to instantly write down in normal Arabic numerals. Trainees were required to do lots of these exercises within strict time limits, so that they gradually became quite proficient at writing down long series of numbers on the service logpads under pressure. It was a foretaste of what was to come in their radio monitoring work at RAF Batty's Belvedere. Towards the end of their training there was a radio cum technical immersion segment where trainees used and became familiar with the standard radio models, AR 88 and 1475 HF sets. They learnt the technical jargon, message codes and so on, necessary for their covert signals work in Hong Kong. In fact, the final end of course examination[9] did include a short test on this technical side of things.

The initial method of language teaching as enshrined in the US education manuals was extremely functional, with a huge emphasis on aural practice, a lot of oral drilling, and varied speaking and conversational exercises. All good common-sense! As the course progressed and the students' language level improved then more translation work into and from G.R. appeared. John Norrish felt that his experience of learning Chinese in the RAF had helped to shape his interest in languages and linguistics, which constituted his life thereafter and included many years lecturing at the Institute of Education, University of London. In retrospect, he looks at the theoretical context of the methodology of RAF Chinese language teaching from a professional viewpoint:

> The overall approach to teaching methodology on the Chinese course was quite eclectic, covering a range of methods, including

basic Grammar and Translation, the 'Direct Method' (involving no translation) and the newest theoretical approach, the 'Audio-Lingual Method'. In the 1940s and 1950s the normal services approach, especially on the language courses in the USA (cf. Earl Stevick and others) was based on behaviourist psychology and structural linguistics, commonly referred to as the 'Audio-Lingual Method'; scholars such as Skinner in psychology and Bloomfield in linguistics had produced what they referred to as 'the first scientific approach to language teaching'. Its main approach was to drill orally structures and vocabulary 'in order to form appropriate habits', as the view of language learning at that time was essentially that language was a set of habits, one set of which (the first language or mother tongue) would 'interfere with' the new set, the language being learnt. Hence the new set needed to be heavily drilled to overcome this interference and there could be no translation. This method had been successful in the USA on service courses at the Foreign Service Institute during the Second World War, where, naturally, motivation among the learners had been very high. It was far less so in secondary schools after the war, where students reported boredom with the constant repetition, and testing revealed little retention of the target language.

Thus the RAF teaching staff had to cope with a teaching methodology which may have been somewhat different from the way in which they themselves had been taught Chinese. It was essential to have the emphasis on aural work, because the very *raison d'être* of the courses was to produce airmen with high-level listening skills in order to satisfy the radio monitoring requirements of RAF Signals Intelligence. Whether tutors at that time had received any language teacher training is not known but presumably someone at the top had done some reading on the latest theories on language teaching. Bill Mellows (No. 4 Course) can shed some light on this, in a later decade at least. After doing Chinese in his RAF National Service, soon after demob he signed on as a long-term RAF regular, and in the ensuing period he learnt the Russian, Polish and Spanish languages, in that order, and became a qualified linguist and instructor in all three. His last five years of service, from 1977 to 1982, found him as a language instructor at the Languages School at RAF North

Luffenham, and while there he was sent on a two-week posting to RAF Newton for a Ground Instructional Techniques (GIT) course on a Teacher Training Module. He remembers that the language training at North Luffenham took place in two blocks, 'A' and 'B'; 'A' Block was the academic block where students studied the pure language with civilian instructors, whereas 'B' Block was the high security block, where RAF personnel, like himself, taught them the applied use of the language and the specialised terminology needed for the purposes of their future Signals Intelligence duties.

For the Chinese tutors, the permanent presence of romanisation in all the teaching materials was an unexpected hurdle, and none of them ever appeared at ease with it. Often they would supplement written G.R. work with a few added Chinese characters on the board and accompanying digression, which usually perked up the class and the general concentration levels.

Strangely enough, an extreme example of a staff member trying to use the direct method style of teaching came from one of the Chinese tutors. John Norrish remembers that his whole class were completely bemused when this tutor, an older scholar from Shanghai, started walking to the door of the classroom while counting Chinese numbers and continued along the corridor until well out of hearing, and then happily re-appeared still counting. This must have been quite a cultural leap because traditional Chinese education was based firmly on rote-learning and teacher-centred classrooms, with the teacher all-powerful and immovably fixed on the teaching platform. One can only think that because he was teaching in a foreign language and not speaking Chinese, he allowed himself to experiment in this way. The same tutor supplied every member of the first courses with Chinese names, written in impressive calligraphy, based on their surnames but choosing characters with significant meaning, rather than just being a rough transliteration of the English sounds. He also had a valuable hand in familiarising trainees with the Chinese characteristic of not losing face, being quite unwilling to adjust his somewhat fractured English pronunciation under any circumstances.

One spin-off effect quickly appreciated by trainees was that those with names difficult for him to pronounce were avoided in class activities, and so they always got off lightly. Another noticeable trait was his traditional aloofness towards other Chinese tutors, especially Southerners and Cantonese in particular, which seemed to signify a superiority of some kind, and trainees still unversed in the ways of Chinese culture and society could make what they wanted of that little human foible. A relevant Chinese saying remembered by James McMullen (No. 5 Course) is some evidence of regional feelings across the North/South divide: 'Do not fear Heaven, do not fear Earth, but fear a Mandarin-speaking Cantonese.'

The training was pretty intensive in terms of classroom hours which were always maintained at around 30-35 hours per working week, and it was quite general for erks (RAF slang for the lowest ranks) to do some weekly revision and preparation, especially when the regular tests were looming up. Motivation of trainees was reportedly good throughout the programme but at times over the course of the year there were brain saturation periods when everyone needed a break, and even the regular weekend passes were not enough to throw this tiredness off. That was when the course leadership became crucial, and feedback indicates that usually the Officer-in-Charge reacted sympathetically. On the initial courses 'Squaddy' Wright was very understanding, and as an example, at the request of No. 1 Course he organised a day visit to a nearby flying station at RAF Gaydon in Warwickshire, because quite reasonably as airmen they wanted to see real aircraft in action. Sqn Ldr Wright himself knew all about these pressures of studying Chinese, albeit in a more comfortable manner than the erks, because during the early 1950s, he had done an intensive one year course in Chinese at SOAS, University of London, followed by a further two years of language study at the University of Hong Kong.

General pressure on the language students was maintained by regular testing; with the four end of term examinations, which occurred about every eleven weeks, being very significant for survival, although this was never explicitly stated. Allowing for reception, basic training and any leave entitlement, the end of the first term test often coincided with 6 months of RAF service and so trainees were upgraded to Leading Aircraftman (LAC), apparently to mark their examination success. It should be mentioned that linguists had first to achieve LAC and SAC ranks in order to reach the top rank of Junior Technician (J/T) available to them, always provided that there were no blemishes on their service records. The end of the third term test took place after most linguists had served for roughly twelve months, and so again they were elevated to Senior Aircraftman (SAC) rank around that time. Success in the final graduation examination after one year's language training meant reaching the exalted J/T rank and a consequent rise in pay. According to Reg Hunt's airman's pay account on demobilisation in 1957 the J/T weekly pay was £5-12-7d, and this was before deductions of voluntary savings in the amount of 10 shillings and national insurance of 3-11d. In Hong Kong, with an exchange rate of £1 = $16 HK, this would give about $80HK per week. The rank was shown by a single chevron (inverted stripe) on the sleeves of the uniform (in today's RAF it is signified by a four-bladed propellor). Everyone knew that the J/T status was a definite reward for the trainee's labours because anyone failing the final examination stayed at the rank and pay of SAC. However these SACs usually proceeded to Hong Kong with all the others and carried out the same duties there; the RAF were not going to waste the products of their one year training programme.

Peter Shortell (No. 5 Course) remembers that

> ...one of [his] group deliberately failed his J/T examination. He reckoned as a lower rank he would be able to get time off more easily as he was an excellent jazz pianist and wanted to do gigs in Hong Kong. It didn't work. He was initially demoted to LAC from SAC, but finally made it to J/T in Hong Kong, having done exactly the same duties as the rest of us.

Peter then continues with the background to this story:

> There is another part to this: some people had developed techniques for getting the answers to exam questions in advance. For example,

they would get a list of suggested test questions from the wastebasket of one instructor, and get another instructor to help with a translation. By the final exam they had been rumbled. Moreover the oral test consisted of live material for the first time. Everybody failed. Now it cannot be true that 44 intelligent airmen who have regularly passed earlier exams could all fail the final one, unless either the teaching was incompetent (unthinkable) or the exam had been too hard – so they added a figure to everyone's marks. This still left three failures. Two of them complained that this was unfair and were given just enough extra to reach the pass mark. The third was our demotee, of course.

Another surprising story from John Henty was that three of No. 6 Course were transferred to GCHQ instead of going to Hong Kong, because they had minimal time left in their National Service. One of them, Lawrie Cooke, recounts the day when they decided to wear their service issue 'civvies' (civilian clothes) to work, instead of clothes from their own wardrobe. That was the only time they were ever challenged by the guards at the entrance to GCHQ, and he thinks that it was the result of the suspicious-looking, ill-fitting garb that they were wearing. And this was before any James Bond spy thrillers had appeared on screen.

The decision to omit written Chinese characters (ideographs) from the initial language training materials was a logical step because linguists would only be required to perform voice interception work with no demand for them to read or write Chinese. This tied in with a Ministry of Defence (MoD) ruling[10] in the mid-fifties that 'Interpreter' grade classification, open to Commissioned Officers, should be of a higher and more comprehensive language level than the 'Linguist' grade, open to NCOs & Other Ranks only. In practice this meant that 'Interpreters' were to be used more for interpreting work or interviewing native speakers, while 'Linguists' should be mainly focussed on the spoken language only, as they were intended to be radio operators, officially termed 'voice interceptors', collecting data through the medium of radio transmissions. Current intelligence jargon would say that interpreters come under a combination of the HUMINT (Human Intelligence) and SIGINT (Signals Intelligence) classifications, while the linguists would come within the SIGINT category alone. And behind the scenes in the 1950s, ELINT (Electronic intelligence) was emerging as a significant form of intelligence gathering. Another dilemma for the MoD[11] was that National Servicemen after one year's specialised training could only perform a short tour of duty before being demobilised, so the powers that be had to consider the overall cost-benefit of the language courses, but in fact these courses survived right up to the phasing out of National Service in 1961.

On the question of reading and writing Chinese characters Flt Lt Cant had a trick up his sleeve right from the beginning, and this was to offer evening coaching in Chinese characters to any volunteer trainees who were interested; not as a course requirement but as an optional extra for interested bodies, and there was also a long-term incentive of taking the Civil Service Preliminary Examination in Mandarin Chinese. There were two textbooks that could be used for learning Chinese characters, using the medium of English and G.R., both by Professor Walter Simon: *How to Study and Write Chinese Characters* and *Chian Tzyh Keh – 1000 Character Lessons.*[12] Initially there were three takers on No. 1 Course, and they formed a small exclusive cell in a corner of Hut 8 at RAF Wythall, where they were gently humoured by the other inmates as they conferred in whispered clandestine sessions while clutching handfuls of character cards that they had made themselves in order to memorise and get to grips with this non-European form of script. Then, later on in their language programme, all of No. 1 Course trainees had a taste of Chinese characters in their studies. Terry Keyms clearly remembers that a weekly sheet of characters, usually of a flying/ military nature, was handed out to be learnt. His memory suggests only a small number, possibly two to three hundred, and this ties in with the end of term (the third term) exam in June 1956, which had a simple paper into characters (or G.R.) and from characters into English. In reality this meant that any motivated trainees could build on this foundation of Chinese characters, and would have the option of taking the Civil Service Preliminary Examination in Mandarin, if they so wished.

With regard to Joe Cant's three initial students of written Chinese, something must have clicked, because one of them passed both the Preliminary Civil Service exam and the subsequent Intermediate Level, while another passed G.C.E. O Level Chinese, all before the end of their National Service. This must have been very satisfying to Flt Lt Joe Cant to see tangible results from all his extra tuition. Subsequently it seems that even more trainees became hooked on written Chinese, so much so that a total of thirteen trainees from No. 3 Course passed the Preliminary Civil Service examination in July 1957. Similar situations occurred on other courses too; for example, John Henty remembers that he and five others from No. 6 Course passed it in July 1959.

Outside of language learning none of the ex-linguists can recall any political lectures of any kind during the one year courses. This must have been a top level decision as to the philosophy and culture of these training courses; or maybe it was just a laissez-faire approach of leaving it to the officers in charge on the ground. Whatever the reasons, there were no talks or discussions on the political system of the newly established People's Republic of China, and there were no anti-communist diatribes and in fact no anti-Chinese propaganda of any kind. All the RAF leadership and teaching staff appeared to be mildly benign in this area; after all they themselves had been through Chinese language courses in London and/or Hong Kong. In fact when No. 1 Course started in 1955, memories in the UK were still fresh from the HMS Amethyst incident on the Yangtse River in 1949, and the Korean War of 1950-53, during which units of a small British military force, as part of a UN task force, had clashed with the Chinese army and some had been taken as prisoners of war. This war had intensified the Cold War groupings of nations in the world, and it was a time of virulent anti-Chinese activity from the Americans, personified by the alleged action of John Foster Dulles in refusing to shake the hand of Chinese Premier Chou En-lai at the Bandung Conference in 1955. The handshake syndrome is one of the most potent human actions in diplomacy between two sides, and it is still being acted out in political arenas today.

Yet all of this Cold Warfare seemed to have had no obvious or overt influence on the content of the RAF Chinese courses, and the ambiance on the courses was never overtly anti-Chinese – there always seemed to be an underlying respect for Chinese language and culture, and in a practical form there was the fact that several of the NCOs had Chinese wives. Alan Barr (No. 1 Course) remembers listening to the National Anthem of the People's Republic and then being given the English translation; and even today he can still remember some of the words. Informants did not mention any anti-Chinese remarks or feelings amongst their groups but they did report that mildly derogatory terms were used by other British service personnel towards Chinese people in Hong Kong. In return the Cantonese had some pithy expressions to describe foreigners, one old form being *Fan Gwai Lo* roughly meaning 'male foreign barbarian', with the strong traditional connotation of Chinese cultural superiority; this has now been processed through time into the softer form of *Gwai Lo,* which even foreigners now accept and use today. All of this could be seen as being pitched at a playground invective level between two racial groups who had a wary respect for each other.

Sometimes trainees did get a little insight into Chinese society because the teaching manuals contained snippets of background history and social practices that related to the language learning. One example in EM506 is an explanation of the Chinese calendar before and after the founding of the Republic of China in 1911, and a note that Sun Yat-sen became President of the Provisional Government of the Chinese Republic on 1 January 1912. Another example is a brief explanation of the difference between the usage and function of the word 'please' in both languages. The native Chinese instructors themselves were always correct and circumspect about themselves in the classroom, but at social gatherings one or two of them would sometimes reveal the odd tale about their personal life pre-RAF, and why they were not in China. One could generalise and say that their very presence in England may have been a decision forced on them by circumstances and indicated some dissatisfaction with their previous life in their homeland. None of the native Chinese instructors were supervised by any RAF teaching personnel during their classes, which shows a degree of trust on both sides, although it must be appreciated that all the teaching materials were strictly prescribed, and supervision could have been seen as a loss of face for the Chinese teachers. The students themselves were in effect the monitors of the classroom content because anything too indiscreet voiced by the native instructors would have presumably raised questions from the linguists and got back to the leadership; and there is no feedback that any such situation ever arose. One wonders if they had signed any contract of confidentiality that laid down strict injunctions or restrained their actions in any way, or indeed if they were granted Hong Kong resident status or British passports in return for their work for the Crown?

Apart from books, blackboards, gramophone records and tape recordings the only other medium of education was through films, and ex-linguists remember that there were two memorable ones during their National Service, neither of which related to language learning. The first, which was shown during basic training, was on atomic warfare and what to do when under attack, and the other, which was shown prior to embarkation for Hong Kong, was on venereal disease (VD).[13] Everyone agrees that the VD film had the greatest impact on them and admittedly some of the images were fairly horrific. The message was that the dangers of this disease were lurking everywhere on the streets of Hong Kong, and this fact was extremely relevant to the life of the linguists when living there. As confirmation of this, as soon as new service personnel arrived in the Colony they were lectured on the out of bounds areas of Hong Kong and ordered to keep well away.

In a lighter vein, the creative humour of the linguists got to work, and courses set Chinese words to familiar pieces of western music which were sung with great gusto; maybe this was a necessary therapeutic release after being penned up in the cloistered confines of the security compound daily. Or could it have been a reaction against the authoritarian approach by the RAF from a group of young men who did not take lightly to this enforced control of their lives. Perhaps it was just good fun, and certainly an elemental part of the group bonding process.

No. 1 Course (to the tune of the Pas de Deux from Swan Lake):
Jeh geh tzyh ne, jeh geh tzyh ne, jeh geh tzyh ne mei yeou yonq! (G.R. script), meaning 'This character, this character, this character is useless!'
[Words based on Jimmy Chuang's excited efforts to introduce new vocabulary in class when he would repeat several times 'Jeh geh tzyh ne', and all of the class would then chorus 'Mei you yonq!']

No. 1 Course (to the tune of 'Onward Christian Soldiers'):
Huooche jann tzai naalii? Nahlii huooche jann (G.R. script), meaning 'Where is the railway station? The railway station is there.'
[These two sentences occur in Unit 1 of EM506, and must have caught on with the group.]

No. 3 Course (to the tune of Cwm Rhondda; 'Bread of Heaven'):
Woo bwu yaw daw Jonggwo chiuh! (G.R. script), meaning 'I don't want to go to China!'

Notes

1   AIR 28/1291 (RAF Wythall Operations Record Book, May 1951 to December 1955).

2   Copy of EM506 as used by the RAF, in the possession of Mike Grindley, inherited from Joe Cant.

3　　　See Chapter 6, 'Gwoyeu Romatzyh'.

4　　　Hockett/Fang (1944), copy purchased by the authors in 2007.

5　　　Hockett/Fang (1945), copy purchased by the authors in 2007.

6　　　Teaching Manual 'Cloudy Bill', in the possession of Mike Grindley, inherited from Joe Cant.

7　　　See Simon/Lu (1954), Simon (1942-44) and Simon/Chao (1945) in the Bibliography for details.

8　　　Phillips (1948).

9　　　Final examination papers from No. 1 Course, preserved over the years by Geoffrey Russell.

10　　DEFE 10/343 (Services Language Training Committee – Minutes of Meetings and Memoranda, 1956-1958, and Services Language Policy Committee – Minutes of Meetings and Memoranda 1958-1962).

11　　DEFE 10/343.

12　　See Simon (1944a) and Simon (1944b) in the Bibliography for details.

13　　Nowadays termed Sexually Transmitted Diseases (STD).

8

OFFICERS & GENTLEMEN

'And gladly wolde he lerne and gladly teche.'
(Chaucer, Canterbury Tales, Prologue, line 308)

It is very clear from personal reminiscences that the staff and tutors of the Chinese language courses, at their various bases, were virtually all held in high regard by their trainees. This was true of the uniformed staff, despite the fact that they represented the authority that enforced the conscripts' absence from home; the officers' willingness to tolerate minor breaches of service requirements, as well as their occasional active protection of their students from over-zealous disciplinary proceedings, no doubt endeared them to the groups under their command, but beyond that most were generally appreciated. The civilian tutors however made an even greater impression on the students than the majority of the RAF personnel, perhaps because although out of uniform they seemed to be displaced persons and so were seen as having more in common with conscripted servicemen than with the officers, but also because they were the first living introduction to the strange language in which trainees found themselves immersed, and offered a foretaste of the different culture which trainees were about to experience for themselves.

It was never evident, at least to the trainees, how the officers in charge of the courses came to be so, and to what extent, if any, they were involved in the planning of the teaching methods and the appointment of military and civilian staff. From the beginning of the National Service courses until April 1958, Sqn Ldr Wright was clearly the principal organiser, and was remembered by many as the officer who arrived during basic training to conduct the preliminary language tests. John Wright had studied Chinese on the RAF training scheme at SOAS in 1952-3 and later in Hong Kong, but was less well known to the student linguists once they had started their training as he did very little teaching himself, but was seen as a rather avuncular figure in the background.

The officer who is best remembered by all the linguists – perhaps because he was around longer than most – was Sqn Ldr Wright's second in command until he himself took charge of the courses in 1958. Flt Lt 'Joe' Cant, with his twirly moustache and twinkle in his eye, was universally seen as the epitome of the elegant wartime RAF type. There were many tales about him, not all of which are verifiable. But he had indeed been a bomber pilot during World War II, and his Whitley aircraft was shot down over Holland in August 1941. He was captured and subsequently imprisoned in Stalag Luft III (East), located in what is now western Poland, the camp famously remembered for the 'Wooden Horse' and 'Great Escape' episodes, and abandoned by the Germans on 28 January 1945, presumably in the face of the Red Army's advance from the east. Joe's name is recorded on the list of British and Commonwealth prisoners who were dispatched (whether by train or by forced march is not clear) to another camp, Marlag-Milag Nord near Bremen. At some point, so the story goes, Joe fell in with Flt Lt K.H. Tan, a fighter pilot of Chinese origin who had been shot down over France in 1944 and interned as a prisoner of war, but soon escaped and, after recapture, was also sent to Stalag Luft III. Later, as Wing Commander Tan DFC, he became one of the most senior officers in the Malayan Auxiliary Air Force. It seems possible that during their relatively short period of time together, Joe developed an interest in Chinese and began to learn the language from Tan.

After the war ended, the RAF must have recognised Joe's interest in and talent for the Chinese language. As he later told Mike Grindley of No. 3 Course when they met as colleagues at GCHQ, he was in Nanjing in 1947 when the Communist forces were taking over control from the Nationalists. The Royal Navy had maintained its treaty right of passage up the Yangtse River as far as Nanjing, but the advancing Communists were not prepared to tolerate this incursion, and military operations followed the navy's efforts to relieve the British garrison and residents there; this most notorious incident, in 1949, was the downriver escape of HMS Amethyst and the sister ships sent to rescue her.[1]

In their later life, at GCHQ in the 1960s, Mike Grindley got to know Joe a little better, in spite of the latter's natural reticence. Joe regularly worked with the Revd 'Fei' Philips, who had been a Baptist minister in Shandong Province in the 1930s. Mike remembers that nobody ever used the title 'Reverend', but always addressed him as 'Fei', so using his and Joe's Chinese names, Mike referred to the room where these two worked as the 'Fei Zhou Autonomous Region'.

With Joe Cant in overall charge in 1958, Flt Lt Paddy Raine, returning from a spell of duty at Batty's Belvedere – the radio interception outpost in Hong Kong where most of the trainees were headed – became officer in charge of No. 7 Course, with Flt Lt Peter George responsible for No. 6. The latter was no ordinary officer type. In his spare time he wrote detective novels and also, under the pseudonym of Peter Bryant, the original story, 'Two Hours to Doom' (published in the USA as 'Red Alert'), from which the Peter Sellers film 'Dr. Strangelove' was made. Mike Wallace, who was No. 7 Course, recalls:

> Being fairly independent of his RAF salary, [Peter George] could afford to be cavalier in his approach to the force. On parade he was on occasion known to give orders in Chinese, to the utter confusion of other RAF personnel parading with us. I was once brought up before him on a charge for some misdemeanour, which I disputed. He said words to the effect of 'There seems to be some doubt here and doubt must go in favour of the accused – case dismissed'. A truly remarkable man.

86

The respect which the Chinese civilian staff attracted is evident from the string of affectionate reminiscences about them, which persisted throughout the eleven courses. Early courses had the benefit of Mac Soong, a snappily dressed and apparently serious man who revealed a dry sense of humour and who seemed to have a personal commitment to the success of the scheme, and later went over to Hong Kong with some of the trainees. Another was T.T. Chen, a plump, round-faced fellow with spectacles, whom Mike Grindley remembers as 'all gold rims and teeth, trying to learn to drive, roaring along the road to Worth [Matravers] in bottom gear, the instructor alongside tearing his hair out'.

Mike Wallace adds to his pen pictures:

> We had three Chinese nationals as tutors. Jimmy Chuang was fairly mature and was convinced we would spend all our time listening to Chinese government economic broadcasts, and tried his best to teach us phrases like 'the current five-year agricultural plan terminates in the fiscal year 1960-61 and had achieved remarkable and sustained growth in the later quadrants'.

However, he was popular with the students and sometimes went with them to the local pub, where he offered samples of dried squid to go with the beer – they were 'inedible!' (this from Ken Brookes of No. 8 Course). Jimmy had a naughty sense of humour. Joe Cant recalled, to Mike Grindley, 'a big social occasion in the Officers' Mess at Wythall with local dignitaries invited, including the Bishop of Birmingham. [The Bishop] asked all the usual questions', eliciting from Jimmy the fact that he had two children. The Bishop therefore assumed that Jimmy's wife must be at home with them, but was contradicted: 'Oh no, she's here, because we gave the kids two big slugs of gin before we came out'. Slight eccentricity was of course always appealing! Bill Mellows (No. 4 Course) recalls one of Jimmy's favourite sayings: 'English is a very laconic language'. Jimmy later took his caravan to Pucklechurch as his on-site living quarters and remained as a Chinese instructor for several years; in fact he appears on a staff photo of the Languages School at RAF

North Luffenham as late as 1969. Terry Keyms, of No. 1 Course, remembers Mac Soong summing up his two compatriots in excellent English: 'Jimmy Chuang is plebeian while T.T. is patrician'.

Mike Wallace again:

> Mr Chi .... spoke very poor English (all right, not as bad as our Chinese, but he was the teacher) and we spent half the time fathoming out what he meant in between fits of barely suppressed laughter at his utterances – for example, 'weep on' turned out to be a weapon! The best was Terry Jang, a moon-faced charmer who nursed us along and did his best to imbue in us a solid grounding in his mother tongue. He used to get us to make up a story [in Chinese] each person relating a portion before handing over to the airman next to him. The art was to lumber the bloke following as much as possible by, for example, cueing him in with 'hu-ran, yeou i-geh heen dah sheng-in' which meant 'suddenly there was a huge noise ....' Follow that, matey!

There were many other anecdotes about the tutors, who were for the most part regarded with wry affection by their students. James McMullen of No.5 Course in his diary recorded an alternative poetic view of Richard Chi:

> Mr. Chi's delightful lessons more and more subtle and humorous. To reproduce his words does not give the accent, the special delivery and the eyes and smile; just a picture in the mind's eye, so wise and colourful, slippery but bronzed and dignified too. The 'Autumn Chi' ... he could be painted by a really good portrait painter – vivacious subject.

Another member of No. 5 Course, Donald Sutton, adds other impressions, with a somewhat different view of Mr Chi:

> I remember our Chinese instructors with a good deal of affection, and those of us who became teachers, in four cases about East Asia, were more influenced than we could have anticipated. Richard Chi had the most interesting background. Once he told us, without divulging any personal role, of how some people would sell property and stocks

they hadn't yet acquired and make fortunes on the Shanghai stock exchange and elsewhere. Another time he told us the Zen riddle of the goose in the bottle: how do you save the bird without smashing the bottle. We quizzed him for weeks about this in our afternoon [language] drill sessions, never getting the right answer; he would always break into his evasive smile and say nothing, even when we finally guessed that the point was to concentrate our minds, not solve a practical problem in the real world. Later he studied at both Oxford and Cambridge, earning degrees at both places, I believe. He published his Cambridge dissertation under the title of 'Buddhist Formal Logic' [and later] taught at Indiana University, a leading centre of Asian studies.

In a separate note, Peter Shortell mentions that he found out that Richard Chi had been 'living in Shanghai when the Japanese arrived, escaped with his life and nothing else except a large collection of scroll paintings – at first the only job he could get was teaching Chinese for the RAF', but Peter later met him in Cambridge where he had at that time been appointed as a lecturer in Chinese art.

In spite of the situation in which they found themselves, the civilian tutors were often learned in their own right, even if at the time their students were only inclined to make fun of their pronunciation. Ken Brooks of No. 8 Course refers to another tutor, P.T. Lü, as a very erudite man, a recognised authority on T.S. Eliot, who spoke excellent English except that he always pronounced 'bom-ber' with two b's, and spoke of the Chinese polishing the bones of their 'incestors'.

Donald Sutton continues:

> Raymond Hsu was another memorable instructor at Pucklechurch, quite a diffident man but effective in getting across difficult points in our small afternoon classes. He gave extra time to those of us who wanted to learn more Chinese characters. He later got a job teaching Mandarin to Hong Kong students at one of the Hong Kong universities.

Terry Chang [Jang] had the best Mandarin, serious, always on task, very boyish, speaking with what we understood to be a perfect accent. Someone .... recorded him reading at speed and then played it back slowly, revealing the most perfect four tones we had ever heard. He went on to SOAS and helped David Pollard [a student on No. 3 Course] to do a series of tapes for the BBC.[2]

Because most of the tuition was aural/verbal, it was easy for the trainees to make fun of the tutors' and of one another's pronunciation and accent, but this teasing was always taken in good part. With hindsight, one can only agree with Donald Sutton, who concludes:

> I never had the impression that these instructors formed a social group, as the RAF officers did, and they conveyed a sense of being the detritus of civil war, far from home and family, little prospect of returning to China, and not really happy in England. They did not seem to be very well paid. Yet it was one of the best achievements of the RAF language programme to select these men and allow us to spend many hours with them. Besides what they taught us of the language, they were exemplars of Chineseness in many different ways.

Notes

1.   A full account of this episode can be found at *http://uboat. net/allies/warships/ship/3926.html*. According to another version of the story, Joe was himself on one of these sister ships, HMS Black Swan, which came under fire and suffered several casualties while attempting to protect the Amethyst from bombardment from the river bank.

2   David Pollard, of No. 3 Course, went on to specialise in modern Chinese literature and in 1979 was appointed to the chair in Chinese at SOAS once occupied by Walter Simon. He was succeeded in this chair from 1990 to 2002 by Hugh Baker, another member of No. 3 Course.

9

REBEL STUDENTS

'The world is yours, as well as ours, but in the last analysis, it is yours. You young people, full of vigour and vitality, are in the bloom of life, like the sun at eight or nine in the morning. Our hope is placed on you.'

(Mao Zedong, Talk at a meeting with Chinese students and trainees in Moscow, 17 November 1957)[1]

When the full responsibility for Chinese language tuition passed from the traditional academic organisation of SOAS to the internal school of the armed forces, the RAF was by far the major user in the armed services of Chinese linguists. Thus the first course for National Servicemen was set up at RAF Wythall, a station about nine miles south of central Birmingham. Later courses included a few regulars, from the RAF and also from the Army (for more detailed information see Appendix A).

All three services were represented in Wythall but army and navy recruits, in very limited numbers, were members of the Russian language courses whose students were completing their technical training and who were in any case mainly RAF personnel. As no students from other services were included in No. 1 Course and the billets were kept strictly segregated, RAF linguists were scarcely aware of them, but there was in any case little interaction with the Russian linguists who, together with the occasional airman of Polish origin, passed through briefly for technical training on their way from the main JSSL establishment (previously at Bodmin, but recently removed to Crail in eastern Scotland) to postings principally in Germany. Apart from the language school, Wythall was at that time also home to a large contingent of trainee wireless operators, some of whom would receive postings to Hong Kong on completion of their courses.. Thus the arrival of this new element of language training passed with no more notice than that which the Mandarin students gave to the rest of the station.

Geoff Russell recorded the impression that after basic training camp at Hednesford, everything in Wythall seemed to be in miniature, with only a single mess for Other Ranks. However there was a small cinema, a large NAAFI (Navy, Army & Air Force Institute) with café and bar, lounge, reading room, two games rooms, a projection television room and a small fully-equipped theatre. Shortly after the group's arrival there was a station production of 'French Without Tears' – which seemed to indicate an attractively light-hearted and rather cultured atmosphere in the base! There was also a wooden station church, with the spire of Wythall Parish Church just visible over the treetops – the village itself (with a pub) was a short walk or a tuppenny (1p) bus ride away. For more ambitious urban entertainment, it was possible to get into Birmingham and back during an evening.

The Chinese course occupied two huts conveniently situated (from the point of view of late breakfasters) close to the cookhouse. A 'hut' consisted of the standard wooden chalet with a dormitory of about two dozen beds with bedside lockers, plus washroom and storeroom at one end and at the other a small separate room for the NCO in charge of the billet, and a connecting corridor to toilets and showers shared with several other huts. Each hut had its 'senior man', chosen by its occupants, who each morning was supposed to marshal his charges to be marched, in a semblance of military discipline, to the security compound where classes were held.

Once inside the classroom, despite the requirement for airmen and officers to wear uniform, the service atmosphere was largely forgotten as students struggled to master the four tones of what was at that time known as 'Mandarin Chinese' and its novel, though not especially challenging, grammar. During the first few weeks of the course many students felt pressure to perform well, since out of the original thirty-nine trainees up to fifteen were to be selected, according to their performance in the first in-course examination, as officer cadets with the prospect of being commissioned as officers in the reserve (RAFVR) after demobilisation. They would be able to wear civilian clothes for the remainder of their National Service while living in comparatively comfortable quarters in Kensington and attending classes at SOAS, with which the RAF's link had not been completely severed. However, despite this allegedly 'cushy' prospect, this option did not appeal to all who joined the course at the outset, and likewise in later courses even some of the academically more able students declined to be considered for SOAS. They were already destined for university after National Service, and found the prospect of spending a few months living and working in Hong Kong, at that time a remote and exotic destination, much more appealing (and, unlike some later courses, this outward-bound group included no married men with family ties, seeking a home posting). So it was sometime around the end of October or the beginning of November 1955 that the 'SOAS Fifteen' were dispatched to London, and those left behind regrouped into one of the two huts, leaving the second one vacant until April 1956 when No. 2 Course, numbering close to thirty, arrived at Wythall.

Outside the classrooms this group, like most of those that followed, quickly began to gel into a unit with, to some extent, shared interests and a shared attitude to military discipline. All National Servicemen remember the shock – or thrill – of having been thrown together at the start of their service with men of totally different backgrounds, from different parts of the country and with funny accents. The additional factor on long training courses like those for linguists was the possibility of getting to know fellow trainees well, each with their particular tastes and hobbies. Besides learning a variety of scatological songs, several members of No. 1 Course recall their introduction to cool jazz – Dave Brubeck, Gerry Mulligan and Miles Davis – by an enthusiast with a record player, while another small group borrowed the education hut to play classical music – on twelve-inch vinyl disks, brought from home by one of their number. The group's trumpeter was however banished by mutual agreement to the washroom – with the door shut – to carry on his regular practice (later he became Professor of Music at a northern university). The two devout Christians, who were inclined to kneel to pray at their bedsides, although cheerfully accepted by their more heathen fellows, did not make any converts, but others learnt a lot about vice by trying out original mixtures of drinks at the pub down the road.

This was the beginning of the era of surreal radio humour, and the popularity of The Goon Show had an influence. One absurdist diversion was to set up an exclusive club, the 'Society for Painless Living', which with somewhat limited geographical knowledge became the 'Outer Mongolian Branch' – SPLOMB – in which each member was given a nickname supposedly indicating his personality. The Society gave Awards for achievements such as remaining 'recumbent in bed' until five minutes before classes were due to start, and Reprimands for such unworthy causes as learning to play the clarinet, promulgating the sport of weight-lifting and 'giving off the foul odour of industry and conscientiousness'. The Society's 'Scribe', Max Dolby, produced a long rhyming ditty with references to every nember of the course, whilst Steve Fletcher, another instigator of this cult with an enthusiasm for surrealism, led a competition to find the most insoluble riddle (one winner was: 'Why does a mouse if it spins? Because the higher it gets, the fewer') and to invent Dadaistic sayings along the lines of 'The further it is from the urn, the longer the beard'. Of such stuff are poets made!.

All three authors remember that No. 2 Course kept the 'Society for Painless Living' going, but their version changed the geographical location to Inner Mongolia, so that the acronym became SPLIMB (Inner Mongolian Branch). This level of pre-undergraduate humour was typical of the linguist courses, to the members of which such word-play came naturally. A rather more intellectual off-duty setting is described in his diary by James McMullen:

> B and A playing the fiddle in the storeroom; D leaning against the doorway in the twilight reading German poetry aloud; G reading *Aeneid VI* for fun. Palace of culture!

When No. 2 Course arrived, to be billeted in the hut next door to that in which No. 1 Course was settled, a rather cruel welcome was devised. In the early stages the plan had been that selected members of the established group would visit the newcomers with stories of the harsh regime and discipline at Wythall, but the plan became more sophisticated. Peter Gardiner of No. 1 Course, who was an active participant in what was about to happen, takes up the story; he admits that as it took place over fifty years ago, his memory may be a little rusty in places:

> The members of No. 2 Course finally arrived at their new posting, tired and hungry and no doubt looking forward to being left in peace and quiet. They were housed in the hut next to us, and it was decided that a few members of No. 1 Course would go round and make themselves known, and lead them into thinking that they had a tough time ahead with very strict NCOs.

> Preparations for the event had included the borrowing of various items of officer and NCO uniform, to permit the two main stages of the welcome; the first being the introductory talk. Four members of No. 1 Course suitably disguised as two officers, a sergeant and a corporal, entered No. 2 hut and the new intake were stood to attention and told to stand easy – the senior 'officer' then proceeded to give them a pep talk which had only just started when he decided that the room was rather hot, and spoke to one of the airmen along the lines of 'it's rather stuffy in here, open that window there's a good chap!', which was duly done. At the end of the talk, those present were asked if they had any questions, and one unlucky individual had hardly opened his mouth when there was an almighty bellow

from one of the 'NCOs' who made it clear that 'you stand to attention when you address an officer'.

The new group were then advised that there would be a full kit inspection which would follow shortly. A lasting memory of this charade was the look of complete horror and disdain on the face of the 'Pilot Officer' when he lifted a piece of kit from the owner's bed in a way which suggested it was something the cat had brought in.

Finally the new arrivals were dismissed and told they could go to the NAAFI. A little later the relevant members of No. 1 Course (now in their normal uniforms) followed them and were amused to see some of the new course muttering together when they realised that some of the faces around them looked distinctly familiar.

It has to be said that this prank was only possible because, on hearing a little about the plan, Flt Lt Joe Cant, twirling the tips of his moustache without batting an eyelid, suggested that while it was clearly a serious military offence to impersonate an officer, there would possibly be an officer's uniform hanging on a certain hook .... The opening of the window was also significant, because other members of No. 1 Course were able to creep quietly along to the window, out of sight of the inmates, and listen to the unfolding drama inside the No. 2 Course hut.

This rather sadistic hoax became something of a tradition, as one course intake succeeded another. Peter Shortell and fellow-students on No. 5 Course foiled a mock inspection by their predecessors, but pulled off the trick on No. 6 Course, complete with two corporals, a sergeant, a military policeman and an officer, to the extent that, after the imposters all repaired to the NAAFI in civvies, they were still addressed as NCOs until the victims suddenly twigged that they had been victims of an elaborate deception. From the victims' point of view, John Henty of No. 6 Course recalls, on arrival at Pucklechurch:

> Shortly after we arrived, we were all ordered to stand by our beds for a full medical inspection, and collectively forced to undergo the

usual indignities. We should have expected something, but we were green and fell for it. The 'officers' conducting this highly irregular inspection were members of No. 5 Course in borrowed uniforms, acquired by courtesy of [a certain Flight Lieutenant].

John adds that two of these imposters subsequently had very successful careers in the Armed Services and in the legal profession, and were each knighted, and wondered whether they remembered once impersonating officers of Her Majesty's Forces. No. 6 Course in due course got their revenge, by proxy, by giving a similar welcome to their successors, who, as Mike Wallace (No. 7) remembered, played the same trick in their turn on No. 8 Course.

Another exploit of John Henty's group could have had a more serious outcome. As he says:

> For reasons still not entirely clear, but probably due to the innate disregard of authority by most National Servicemen, a number of us were charged with mutiny ... for collectively failing to parade at 7 o'clock one morning outside the billet when ordered to do so by the billet corporal ... to be marched off to breakfast. ... Fortunately the timely intervention of [Flt Lt] Peter George, who seemed to spend much of his year getting his language students out of trouble, saw the charge of alleged mutiny reduced to some lower level misdemeanour, with most of the offenders being given 14 days' 'jankers' [extra work duties as punishment] which for me included the onerous task of washing Peter George's car. I still maintain, as I did at the hearing when paraded before the station C.O., that I was asleep at the time the order was given ... Rumour has it that the C.O. didn't want a mutiny on his station to spoil an unblemished record before his impending retirement.

A rather more colourful version of the episode was given by another member of the course, who recalled that the reason for the early morning parade was that, contrary to regulations, some of the students had arranged to take it in turns to go over to the canteen to collect tea and bacon sandwiches and bring them back to share in the billet. He adds that the NCO concerned was peeved because the preceding night he 'drove into a hole in the road outside the camp where we had moved the red light'. Yet another, Peter Shortell, told how after this episode the group was summoned before 'Squaddy' Wright for a dressing-down but the punishment was no more than to clean the classroom windows – being in a secure area, the windows were rarely cleaned. These stories show the nonchalant attitude of typical linguists, and how they were gently sheltered by their officers.

Similar disrespect for the military aspect was shown by the members of No. 7 Course, as related by Ken Brooks who was in No. 8 Course and therefore their junior, when they appeared on parade in pyjamas, or with bowler hats, umbrellas and briefcases (this must have been the normal daily muster from the billets to the classrooms, not a parade ground affair!)

It was nevertheless made clear that there were limits to the tolerance of non-military behaviour, as related by Mike Grindley. A routine duty in Pucklechurch was night guard at the Armoury, with two airmen on duty. On one occasion one of the two went off to the NAAFI to get something – this was permissible as long as his companion remained locked inside the Armoury. However the man left behind fancied a cigarette so stood to smoke in the open doorway – unfortunately the strongly-sprung door closed, leaving him on the outside. The hapless airman was discovered, court-martialled, and spent time in Colchester military prison before being re-assigned.

* * * * * * * *

So it was that in September 1956 members of the first course passed their final examinations and graduated as Junior Technicians – smartening themselves up for a passing out parade which got under way only after the station commanding officer, who had slightly overindulged the night before, was rousted from his bed to come and take the salute – and then left on their embarkation leave, never to return to classrooms surrounded by wire fences.

98

With their departure the second Chinese course was able to return to Wythall to complete its training and to be replaced, at RAF Worth Matravers on the picturesque Dorset coast, by members of No. 3 Course, who would remain there until facilities at Pucklechurch were ready. For those wishing to pay regular visits on 36-hour passes to their homes in the Midlands or North, Worth might not have been an ideal location, but with its peaceful rural surroundings and relatively relaxed service discipline many regarded it as a dream posting. It was a very small station, one of the original radar camps where, as Peter Treacher says, the Chinese language school was the main element and there was a strong *esprit de corps* among the trainee linguists. Perhaps the fact that the officer in charge of the course – still Sqn Ldr Wright – outranked the Station Commander had something to do with this.

John Norrish describes life in two wooden huts, with a coal-fired stove in the middle of each and ablutions and toilets in a separate building. For a few short months the students led an idyllic life: local swimming in good weather, 'for female talent by bus to Swanage – den of iniquity!' says John Norrish, who joined a local music singing group, and went with them around nearby villages to perform in various concerts.

Peter Treacher noticed that discipline tightened up when, in the spring of 1957, the School moved to a more typical service way of life in RAF Pucklechurch, with a distinctly less relaxed regime and regular station parades. Bill Mellows, who was at Pucklechurch on No. 4 Course, remembers cold draughty pay parades in a big hangar, scruffy billets, 'bull' nights spent cleaning the barracks' windows, floor bumpers with smelly polish and walking around on felt pads for the rest of the week to avoid scuffing the floor. On the other hand, good communication links for trips home at the weekends were generally appreciated, and Mike Wallace who joined No. 7 Course there found it was 'like home' compared to his basic training camp at Bridgnorth. And the old balloon hangars were perfect as badminton courts!

However, the vagaries of service discipline sometimes caught up with airmen, particularly anyone who was looking for a 'skive' (an easy option). On the first Sunday morning 'church parade', Mike relates,

> the Flight Sergeant in charge called for all Methodists to fall out, followed by Congregationalists, Jews and atheists. When he got to agnostics, I decided that was near enough for me and I joined the small throng. Bad choice! because the Flight Sergeant then had enough 'volunteers' for kitchen cleaning and the group scrubbed up in the kitchen while the rest took it easy in church.

Another correspondent notes how he (legitimately) visited the Pleasure Ground in Blackpool wearing uniform, and took off his beret on the Big Wheel to avoid its blowing away – on his descent he was met by a Military Policeman who put him on a charge for being improperly dressed. The charge followed him all the way to Hong Kong, but was eventually dismissed.

A very few students tried to 'work their ticket' to escape from National Service by acting mad – or at least, their colleagues seem to have presumed the performance was planned. Thus a man on No. 3 Course who was unhappy was said to have read up on mental illnesses then acted them out, cutting holes in his greatcoat and complaining that the mice had got at it, and appearing on parade ill-dressed. On a later course, a man used to draw chickens on the wall of the billet, then brought back food from the mess to throw to them. It appears that these men did get taken off the courses, but whether because of insanity or for some more earthly reason is not clear.

Throughout National Service, many servicemen went back to family or girlfriends by means of hitchhiking. This practice was far more common than nowadays, and by travelling in uniform servicemen were generally guaranteed lifts without too much waiting about. John Henty again:

Pucklechurch virtually emptied at the weekend, with a sizeable contingent heading for the A4 to hitch to London, returning generally by the same means in the early hours of Monday morning. Snow forced me on one occasion to abandon the journey in Marlborough, where a reasonably comfortable night was spent in the rather upmarket all-night public conveniences, before staggering mid-morning into class without Flt Lt George so much as batting an eyelid!

There was a repeated plea from linguists based at non-flying camps to see a working airfield, and very occasionally the request was acceded to. James McMullen was lucky enough to be offered a place on a training flight for experience, but remembers little more than sitting on the floor of the aircraft for about eight hours, wearing a parachute and making cheese sandwiches for the crew.

In September 1959, during No. 8 Course, the Chinese school moved to Tangmere, and the three final courses in which National Servicemen were included, and which had much reduced numbers, were based there. At Tangmere the School was a small unit in a 'proper' RAF base with real aircraft and a runway, and it remained the training camp for linguists until the end of the courses for National Servicemen. Here the accommodation was better, in three-storey buildings rather then wooden huts, but a certain amount of service duty (as opposed to classroom work) was required. Ken May, who was with No. 11 Course, remembers that Monday night was 'bull night' (an evening spent on domestic chores), there were occasional CO's parades 'at dawn' for the whole camp, and occasional overnight guard duty. This involved patrolling a set route with torch and whistle, two hours on and four hours off, with unofficial stops in the boiler room where the civilian worker provided tea and company. On one such duty at the weekend, Ken with two others reported a small chimney fire, the fire brigade was called and later the airmen were commended by the duty sergeant and duty officer (neither of whom, of course, was around at the time!) But Ken's abiding memory is of the three mile walk back to camp 'after closing time on pay night, [which] was to become a regular feature of our year in Sunny Sussex'... Keith Drury also remembers the so-called walk back to barracks, as he and two others were given 'jankers' for a week after upsetting the locals by singing all the way home from the pub at 3 a.m. (whether the pub stayed open specially, or whether they were singing for three hours, he does not relate.) Keith added that the 'fatigues' involved working from 6 to 8 p.m. then reporting to the guardhouse at 10 p.m., which left two hours drinking time as long as they didn't blow on the Military Police at 10 p.m.!

For the select groups of National Servicemen who found themselves being drafted as officer cadets to pleasant quarters in Kensington with daily classes at SOAS, there was perhaps less obvious reason to grumble. Besides being better paid (£7 a week all found!), having season tickets on the London Underground and vouchers for lunch available at the Air Ministry canteen, they were provided with civilian clothes which they were able to wear most of the time. As David Raderecht (1955-57) says, the servicemen living in Queensgate Terrace were obliged to put on uniform only while on door duty, which arose about once every two months. The cadets were expected to make their own beds, but had no other domestic duties.

The course work for RAF cadets at SOAS remained an extension of the regular academic course, with additional spoken Chinese classes but with a curriculum which 'included sessions on grass script and Chinese poetry – not perhaps the most useful for the RAF's purposes', said John Hampson (SOAS 1953-55), but went on to add: 'As a recent graduate in English literature and art history from Toronto University, I was delighted by this cultural input and it made a change from the recurrent propaganda in the Chinese press about "the running dogs of the Americans".'

It seems that there was little planning over what to do with the cadets during academic vacations – Don Rimmington (1955-57) spent vacation time at two or three RAF bases, one on the coast of

Pembrokeshire where there was ample time to spend on the beach, but another where the Commanding Officer declared that the cadets' hair was too long and they all were obliged to have a haircut on the spot. Towards the end of their National Service each cadet group was sent on a three-week Officer Cadet Training Unit (OCTU) course. The tests there included the naming of RAF bomber aircraft and drilling the rest of the group on the parade ground; Don Rimmington, who passed out in 1957, noted that some cadets were unable to do one or other of these tasks, but nobody failed the course. So, with the success of their enforced military careers, quite possibly none of the Chinese linguist officer cadets regretted the lost opportunity of a trip to the Far East!

Notes

1   From *Quotations from Chairman Mao Tsetung* (Peking: Foreign Languages Press, 1972), Section 30 -Youth, p. 288.

10

SO MANY STAGING POSTS

'What use is it to stare out sadly over the balcony railing?
There are so many staging posts between here and home.'

(Lines from poem by Du Mu, AD 803-852)

For some years after World War II the RAF was still using troopships
to ferry men out to bases beyond Germany, with travel to the Far
East taking up to seven weeks.[1] A student on one of the earlier SOAS
courses, who subsequently went out for a spell in Hong Kong in
the early '50s, remembers the voyages, particularly his return to
Britain aboard the famous *Empire Windrush*.. However the use of
sea transport faded rapidly during the 1950s and had ceased entirely
by the end of National Service. By 1955, the RAF was beginning
to charter planes from Airwork Ltd. and other companies flying
Avro Yorks, Douglas Dakotas, Vickers Vikings and Handley Page
Hermes passenger aircraft. The Suez crisis in 1956 had the effect of
expanding civilian charters, because several of the transit countries
no longer permitted military planes to stop over or even overfly
their territories.

Nevertheless, and perhaps because of the small size of the course
groups, each of which was needed to replace another small group on
the job in Hong Kong at a fairly definite time, the travel arrangements
for linguists often seemed a bit haphazard. But as the years went by,
military transport arrangements just like civilian travel improved
both in speed and comfort.

Members of No. 1 Course flew out from the UK in three small groups a few days apart in October 1956. Geoff Russell kept a diary at the time. He noted that, after a night at Clyffe Pypard, the tiny transit camp near RAF Lyneham in Wiltshire, his group was due for an early morning start on the first day of their 9000 mile journey; but they were unable to get breakfast because no cooks were awake – not an auspicious start. Later, passing through the departure gate, a kindly Customs officer offered to sign return vouchers for any valuables they might be carrying – but all the baggage kit had gone on ahead, including the keys!

This outward journey was by Transport Command Handley Page Hastings, a post-war troop carrier which held about 40 seats in double pairs, all facing backwards. Its cruising speed was 230/240 knots at between ten and twelve thousand feet, and it rumbled on steadily for eight hours or so until it had to stop, and its passengers – almost all of whom had never left England before – had a fairly sleepless night in a strange bed in a hot barrack room in a strange country followed by another early start next morning.

The first night was in Castel Idris near Tripoli, named after Libya's then reigning monarch. The base had previously been called Castel Benito after Mussolini, and during World War II had been a paratroop training school and base for the 5th Air Squadron of the Italian Air Force – that old name was still visible on some of the buildings. Could it nowadays be called Castel Gaddhafi? Whatever the associations of the name, the place came as a pleasant surprise – an RAF transit hotel in pale pink, with round arches and palm trees and ceiling fans in the dormitories – and whisky available for 6d a tot (less than 2½p), best cigarettes 1s 3d (7½p – about a quarter of the then current price in the UK). Here the linguists changed for the first time into the tropical kit with which they had been issued in the UK. The official term for this dress was KDs (Khaki Drill), and it consisted of sandy-coloured short-sleeved shirts and shorts, which linguists wore for most of their stay in Hong Kong except for a brief time during the cooler winter months.

The second night in Habbaniyah, near Baghdad, was a disappointment after this; tented accommodation near a lake on a barren plain, but with security lax enough to allow a continuous procession of herdsmen and goats to pass nearby. At night there was the constant chatter of crickets and the yapping of dogs – or allegedly, as Geoff Russell's diary records, jackals – which provided some sport as occasional hunting parties sallied out from the camp. Another group arriving here found the heat so overpowering that they all volunteered to have a haircut! – in a bell tent with a friendly Iraqi barber. Travelling with No. 3 Course, Mike Grindley regretted – fifty years later – that he had not accepted the offer of a Habbaniyah taxi driver to take a trip to Baghdad – but it would have been a fifty-mile round trip across the desert in the dark, and the risk of missing the transport plane next morning was too great. A consolation for him the following day was flying across northern India, with views of the Himalayas on the horizon.

On the way to the next destination, RAF Mauripur in Pakistan, the Hastings carrying some of No. 1 Course caused a certain amount of anxiety when, off the Baluchistan coast, it lost power in one of its four engines – but it eventually arrived to make a normal landing. This group had to wait in Mauripur for thirty-six hours whilst a replacement engine was flown out from England, but Keith Scott records that, a year later whilst awaiting repatriation from Changi, he was reassured to see a similar Hastings making test passes overhead on just one engine. They were pretty rugged aircraft, ideal – except for speed – for the kind of work they had to do and the conditions under which they operated.

The enforced stay at Mauripur provided some with entertainment in the form of a stream of vendors coming into the camp to hawk carved ivory ornaments, embroidered fabrics, and to the young men's innocent eyes, all the treasures of the East – but much more expensive than in Libya. Others found it less pleasant. Another Hastings, carrying some of the course members, as a result of a runway obstruction in Mauripur had to make an unplanned stop in

106

Karachi. As this was an entirely civilian airport and the passengers were all in uniform, they had to stay in the plane sitting on the baking runway whilst local airport officials boarded and fumigated them with spray guns – presumably to kill all the wicked bugs they had picked up in North Africa or Iraq. After a long hot day, Geoff Russell found Mauripur wasn't worth waiting for – brick huts containing absolutely nothing except beds and ceiling fans – but the next overnight stop, Negombo in Ceylon (Sri Lanka) was much more attractive. All the billets there were just half-walled with verandahs and woven bamboo curtains, giving the novice travellers the idea that they were moving into ever more exotic lands.. This building style almost made up for the variety of insect life which lived inside the barracks – including the threat of scorpions under the beds and in one's shoes. But there were lots of little shops and stalls just outside the camp gates, and meeting local residents for the first time, whether in Pakistan or in Ceylon – despite the fact that they were just stall-holders looking for a quick buck – reinforced the sense of impending oriental adventure.

This travel excitement was intensified for some by arrival in Changi, near Singapore, for a 48-hour break. After buying a T-shirt which he could wear with tropical uniform shorts so as to pass as a civilian, Geoff Russell went with a few others to explore Singapore, and remembered a few other 'firsts' – first proper Chinese meal, first acquaintance with cinema air-conditioning (the film was 'The King and I' on its first release) and a tentative (because impecunious) exploration of the famous Raffles Hotel.

The final leg to Hong Kong was by a rather older aircraft, an RAF Vickers Valletta – a twin-engined development of the Wellington bomber, used as troop transport and also to carry paratroops, and affectionately known as the Flying Pig. There was a degree of apprehension as it first stopped to refuel at Tan Son Nhut airport in Saigon, then in an uneasy peace after winning independence from the French, and at last made the final touch-down, after six days flying, in what was then universally recognised to be one of the most hazardous airports in the world, between the apartment blocks and washing lines which surrounded the old city centre airport at Kai Tak in Kowloon.

On leaving Hong Kong for demobilisation in mid-1957, some of the group who made that six-day flight out made the return journey from Singapore to the UK in 17 hours flying time, with one refuelling stop, but also with a certain amount of trepidation – by RAF Comet.[2]

Although this was still exceptional, by the time of No. 3 Course the normal journey time had already shortened by several days. Peter Treacher remembered flying by BOAC Argonaut (a DC4 derivative, and the plane on which the young Queen Elizabeth flew back from Kenya in February 1952 after the death of her father) via Rome, Istanbul, Basra, Karachi, Calcutta and Bangkok, with overnight stops in Basra (at the Shatt al-Arab Hotel) on the way out and Karachi on the way home.

In due course the flight got even shorter – though not necessarily less exhausting. By the time that Ken Brooks travelled with No. 8 Course in 1960, the overall journey time had diminished to a shattering twenty-eight hours, by Bristol Britannia from Brize Norton. This experience was shared by No. 11 Course, including refuelling stops at Ankara, Karachi, Bombay and Rangoon, but no overnight stays – as Keith Drury recalls, 'each stop hotter than the last' which made him wonder whether Hong Kong would be even hotter and how anyone could possibly cope.

This transport evolution was not however consistent – Mike Wallace on No. 7 Course flew out on a De Havilland Comet, but returned in 1960 as far as Singapore by an old, noisy RAF Hastings – only to find that he and his companions were not booked onto any ongoing transport, and abandoned in the holding unit known as Pool Flight – 'a depressingly huge and silent barrack block where it was easy to imagine the skeletons of airmen consigned here and never heard of again'. After days of pestering the Flight Office, Mike and his companions got seats on a returning Bristol Britannia – an aircraft nicknamed the 'Whispering Giant', but on this occasion not living up to the reputation because it was full of service families with 'dozens of kids condemned to fifteen hours of confinement'. Fortunately his fiancée was waiting for him on his arrival in the UK.

There were however times when the RAF still wanted to test an airman's sea legs, and various members of linguist courses returned to the UK by troopship. This provided a different experience, because there were military families aboard with children under the age of 12, who consequently were required by law to continue their education whilst afloat. Responding to a call for teachers – or intending teachers – linguists evidently had the right attributes, and a number of them found themselves spending their voyage giving instruction to small groups of children on a variety of subjects, whilst avoiding the tedium and chores of the other troops. John Henty on No. 6 Course describes leaving Hong Kong on the *Empire Fowey* (a 1936-built German passenger ship, which had been seized at the end of the war and travelled widely as a British troopship) for the four-week journey home, and as his 'heavily exaggerated experience of helping out in a Sunday School was enough to satisfy the interviewer', he found himself with fellow-linguist Phil Cline, both smartly dressed in their tropical gear with 'very smart' service-issue sunglasses, sent topsides to educate the children of officers, and taking part, before the ship's arrival at Southampton, in an official Speech Day with distribution of certificates. One of the highlights of the trip remembered by John Henty was docking in Colombo where he illegally exchanged his ten shilling notes for 5 half-crowns (25% profit); a lowlight was Aden which was as he described it in a letter home, 'all dust and rock and the most uninteresting place I have ever been to'. But at least the voyage in 1960 was a little shorter than a couple of years earlier, as the Suez Canal had by then been reopened

Although the members of No. 1 Course travelled to Hong Kong in RAF uniform, all the later groups were able to pretend – at least during the journey – that they were not really conscripts at all. The most usual form of transport thereafter was by civilian airline, stopping at civilian airports, so there was an obligation to travel in civilian clothes – with kit-bags, as Mike Prada remembers, turned inside out to supposedly hide the military insignia. Another advantage was each being issued with a full British passport, with employment entered as 'Government officer'. Many groups seem to have enjoyed this privilege. By the time that John Henty of No. 6 Course was sent on his mission to save Hong Kong, transport was arranged in a chartered BOAC Bristol Britannia, flying by way of Istanbul, Karachi, Bombay and Bangkok. Unfortunately – or happily as John puts it – long-haul flights were still problematic. An engine failure in Karachi meant that the group was forced to spend a week at the then run-down and infamous Minwallah's Grand Hotel close to the airport. A break from routine, except that by the fourth day the whole party had succumbed to that combination of heat and unaccustomed food and drink that leads to 'the dreaded squitters' – not before an enterprising local barber had made a fortune in one day by carrying out about a hundred crew cuts. However they eventually reached the final destination, which had till then been only a fantasy; as John Henty poetically declared: 'We arrived at Hong Kong early in the morning and, looking out of the window as we made our approach, the sight of junks moving lazily across the still moonlit waters between the islands was something out of this world'.

On some arrivals the group stayed kicking its heels in Kai Tak for a day or two while most went directly across the bay by motor launch towards Little Sai Wan, the RAF base on the eastern tip of Hong Kong Island. When Keith Scott's group arrived, there had been serious rioting during the preceding few days, apparently sparked by the tearing-down of a Nationalist (KMT) flag by Communist sympathisers, and the whole colony was under curfew and appeared unusually quiet. However, although hampered by their 80lb apiece of baggage, the group only had to make the short distance from the aircraft to a wharf on the edge of the airfield to board a launch for North Point, on the Island, where transport awaited for the short ride into the base. The apparent peace in the streets of the city was shattered on arrival at the barracks at Little Sai Wan, where they were met by the traditional jeers from the balconies, and cries of 'Get some in!' from self-styled veterans who had suffered the same jibes on their own arrival a few months earlier. Three years later, Mike Wallace got off the plane at Kai Tak, walked to the edge of the runway, down some steps and into the motor launch, to be whisked away through the harbour and the Lyemun Gap direct to the jetty at Little Sai Wan. Many years later he recalls that he never had a flight arrival at any airport as easy as that.

All of these minor adventures, which to today's seasoned traveller seem no more than skimming the surface of travel experience, were utterly novel to young men in the 1950s. As the decade wore on, and National Service was approaching its end, the average age of conscripts increased and a few had made youthful excursions into nearby Europe; but a far larger number knew little more about foreign parts than they might have picked up from casual glances at National Geographic magazines, or have seen in a black and white Pathé newsreel in the cinema. Very few who lived in the provinces had been to London (and vice versa). Even fewer, at the time of call-up, had been anywhere near an aeroplane. It is hard to imagine nowadays the impact – the utter strangeness – of these crowded experiences on the small coterie of conscripts who had been selected, sworn to secrecy, and thrown into totally different non-European cultures. Some delighted in the strangeness, some tolerated it, but virtually all felt that it changed their outlook on life, even if not their subsequent career. We shall return to this theme in Chapter 13.

Notes

1   Hickman (2004).

2   The de Havilland Comet 1, operated by BOAC, was the world's first pure jet passenger aircraft. It made its inaugural flight from London to Johannesburg on 2 May 1952.

Following a series of disastrous accidents in 1953-4, in which a total of over 100 died, it was withdrawn from civil services. After intensive investigation and development the Comet 4 returned to passenger service in 1958. Meanwhile the RAF took delivery of several Comet 2s at Lyneham in 1956, for use as troop transports (*http://news.bbc.co.uk. onthisday/dates/stories/may/2*, also *http://dnausers.d-n-a. net/dnetGOjg/disasters.htm*).

11

KEEN SPIRITS

'In the morning, spirits are keen; later in the day they begin to falter; in the evening, thoughts turn to home.'

(Sunzi, Art of War, 7.21)

The day of arrival at Little Sai Wan base was taken up, as always on posting to new barracks, with administrative chores – the allocation of rooms, the issue of bedding, the checking of equipment – and finding one's way around, which normally implied the exploration of the NAAFI, the camp cinema, and so on. The accommodation was a surprise, after experience of barracks in Britain and on the journey; spartan but neat and newly built four- or six-bedded rooms with balconies, in blocks that were named after famous RAF officers – Trenchard, the first Chief of Air Staff and virtual founder of the RAF, war heroes Cheshire and Gibson, and 'Bomber' Harris. All these normal pre-occupations were however overshadowed by the shocking discovery that all servicemen had servants! This is how it seemed, when incomers realised that for each group of rooms there was a Chinese *amah* – usually a local woman from the nearby tenement blocks – who cleaned the room and did laundry. For a Hong Kong dollar or two (a few pence in today's coin) the amah would take a shirt or a pair of trousers in the evening and have it back cleaned and pressed early next morning. Besides the room amahs, there was a woman, or maybe several women, naturally known as 'Sew Sew' who would on request re-attach buttons or carry out small repairs to uniform or civilian clothing. There was of course a good deal of speculation about whether the amahs might provide additional personal services, but in fact this was by and large nothing more than standard servicemen's gossip. Mostly the amahs maintained a smiling but respectable distance, although over the years there was a handful of regular airmen who overcame the cultural divide to set up homes with Chinese women. Even fewer married – having to overcome strong official RAF disapproval – and returned eventually to the UK. with families. Max Dolby of No. 1 Course recalls how, when he was working in local government in Peterborough a few years after National Service, he held open a door in the Town Hall for a young woman with a baby, and suddenly recognised her as an amah from Little Sai Wan who had married a corporal.

Besides the amahs, a handy source of unforeseen needs, such as swimming trunks and other small items – though not as cheaply as in town – was discovered by some airmen: a quick-repair service tailor known as Abdul who could often be found at his stall at the foot of one of the stairwells. Another useful man, a Cantonese who worked alone in the stores, was willing to truant from his workplace in order to give lifts into town in his own car, undercutting the fare charged by local taxi drivers (who were well aware that servicemen going out of Little Sai Wan were in no position to bargain).

However impressed the new arrivals were by the comparative luxury of the Sai Wan billets, this was eclipsed by the first visit to their work location on top of the Peak. To begin with, the journey from the Eastern end of Hong Kong island, where Little Sai Wan was situated, rattling through the overcrowded streets of North Point, Wan Chai, Causeway Bay and Central Victoria, then up to the top of the Peak where the workplace was, took over an hour each way by three-ton lorry (or, in comparative luxury a few years later, by minibus). Such lorries were known in the Anglo-Indian lingo adopted by the British Forces throughout Asia as *gharries* The journey itself was an adventure. Shortly after leaving the base, the gharry would plunge into the bustling, noisy streets, bouncing along between the ceaseless trams and other vehicles of all sizes and ages, bicycles, taxis, rickshaws and trotting porters (in the years before political correctness, normally referred to as coolies) carrying an enormous variety of goods on shoulder poles. The typical city din was enlivened by unrestricted horns, bicycle bells, shouts and the clamour of Chinese pop music from local bars. Eventually the truck would begin to climb out of this maelstrom, up surfaced but narrow and steeply winding roads, as the packed streets gave way to detached villas with ornate and beautifully kept gardens, the homes of British colonial families, European businessmen, diplomats and Chinese entrepreneurs, up to where the houses were increasingly separated from each other by luxuriant tropical foliage, and further up to a small asphalted turning place where the truck finally stopped.

There was then a footpath winding up through tall green undergrowth, which though in reality was only a few dozen yards seemed like at least half a mile (especially as the duty watch had to carry its own rations and other paraphernalia), until one emerged at the site of the activity for which all the previous year's study, the examinations, the military discipline, the unforeseen camaraderie, the lugging of kitbags on and off planes and boats, had been a preparation. Officially known by the rather charming title of RAF Batty's Belvedere,[1] the linguists' place of work was a couple of single-storey concrete blocks surrounded by radio aerials, on the summit of The Peak, the highest point on Hong Kong Island. Elsewhere these mundane surroundings would have been a dispiriting place to spend eight hours a day on constant shiftwork, but here the location was breathtaking. The arrival of each new draft of linguists, fresh from their classroom year in the drab UK, was normally in early autumn or early spring, which in Hong Kong were inclined to be the best times of the year. Standing outside the buildings on a sunlit early morning, each draft of newcomers arriving for their first duty shift found the panorama of the whole colony laid at their feet (though unfortunately not visible from inside their workplace). The multi-storeys of Victoria, the Bank of China just overtopping the Hong Kong & Shanghai Bank for pride of place as the city's tallest, the massed blocks of tenement housing, stood it seemed almost vertically below. Beyond them lay the eternally busy harbour, with the Star Ferry boats, all sizes of heavily laden junks and sampans, and the occasional British or American naval vessel standing grey in this medley of colour. From far above the melée, it was possible to forget the fumes and smells and to understand why the name of the colony had the meaning of 'Fragrant Harbour'.

Across the water, sheltering in the bay, lay the other half of the city of Hong Kong – Kowloon with its dockyards, warehouses and equal bustle, where one could watch from above the touch-downs and take-offs of aircraft from Kai Tak airport where the linguist group had arrived, dropping in between the washing lines of the tenement blocks, a day or so earlier. Later, when the opportunity arose to explore beyond the city into the New Territories, they would discover townships scattered between vegetable plots and paddy fields, stretching towards the mysterious blue hills which represented the forbidding border with the People's Republic.

It had been suggested to men on No. 1 Course, back in the UK, that they see the film *Love is a Many Splendored Thing*, newly released in 1955, to get an impression of what the city looked like. William Holden took the lead and the Eurasian leading lady was portrayed by Jennifer Jones. The camera shots of Hong Kong in the film were very impressive, but actually being there was altogether different. For most service personnel who spent time at this isolated unit in a corner of the British Empire, the panoramic outlook looking down on the harbour – one of the most famous picture postcard views in the world – never ceased to inspire. Incidentally, the film is a marvellous historical record of the almost vanished Hong Kong of half a century ago. Yet another Hollywood film, revealing the penurious and sleazy side of Hong Kong was made several years later, *The World of Suzie Wong*, and Mike Prada (No. 6 Course) remembers going into town to watch street scenes being shot – he knew one of the cameramen; again William Holden was the leading actor and this time his love interest was a Chinese actress, Nancy Kwan.

Batty's Belvedere must have been one of the smallest RAF camps in existence. In early days there had been a signals station established on the Peak by the Royal Navy in the late nineteenth century, but at some unknown time it had been acquired by the RAF; and in 1956 it consisted of some radio masts and a small one storey main building plus outbuildings. Inside there was a series of radio sets spaced at intervals along the wall and around the central table, with a room at the end for the watch officer who was in charge of the station for each eight hour duty. One side of the workplace was staffed by male native Chinese operators and the other by RAF personnel, and although there were rare exceptions such as when No. 6 Course were at Batty's,[2] there was virtually no socialising between them after work, as each group returned to their different lives and interests. The thought may have arisen in the minds of some linguists about the trustworthiness of Chinese personnel in this high security radio unit[3] (where the only cleaners to be employed were allegedly local deaf and dumb Chinese),[4] but theirs not to reason why, and the combined memories of ex-linguists place the Chinese in small groups drinking tea and chatting a lot of the time. This impression might have been exaggerated because they were obviously in the charge of the RAF Officer in command, although as foreign civilians their contractual obligations presumably could not bind them as closely to the national security of the UK as did the commitment of the conscripted RAF linguists. Some ex-linguists had the vague memory that the Chinese operators were promised a British passport for their services to the Crown, but no confirmation of this is available today. However during the day shifts, when the Chinese were around, the atmosphere at Batty's seemed lighter and more relaxed. Many linguists retain a memory of one Tommy Harrison who seems to have been a leader of the Chinese group throughout this period; a bulky Anglo-Chinese whose mother was from Shanghai and whose father was a merchant seaman. According to Ken Brookes (No. 8 Course), Tommy later went into the shoe trade, and in typical Chinese fashion he would measure up for made-to-measure shoes by having the customer put bare feet on two pieces of newspaper and draw around them. In later years Tommy came over to England to see his family, and met up with some of his British linguist ex-colleagues.

Outside the main building, and just within the barbed wire perimeter fence there was an even smaller block that served as cookhouse, where during the daytime a Chinese cook made 'snacks' to order, or knocked up extremely bland meals from RAF rations (the civilians were known to provide their own thermos flasks of rice!). There were facilities for do-it-yourself food preparation because in the early days on 'night bind' there was no cook. There are many anecdotes about the nocturnal meals of boiled potatoes or even chips with tinned steak and kidney cooked by young national servicemen without any previous culinary experience. But at night the atmosphere at Batty's became more menacing. The relatively isolated position, on the highest point of the island, led to a variety of ghost stories. The tales mainly concerned the supposed last allied soldier to be killed in the wartime defence of Hong Kong – or alternatively the last Japanese soldier to be killed in the re-occupation of Victoria Island who now roamed the Peak headless. Such superstitions were best ignored by young linguists walking through the dark undergrowth on their way to night watch, but they were not above spinning the stories to the more superstitious of their Chinese colleagues, and most airmen cannot recollect any Chinese operators, cooks or cleaners being around during night duty. According to Mike Prada there was for a time a Chinese cook on duty up there, but one night, working by candlelight, he saw a ghostly figure outside the camp's barbed wire fence, and ran terrified into the main building, never to do night duties again.

After 1957 a second storey was added to the main block, with the upstairs floor apparently a basic intelligence room with maps for plotting purposes, and normally out of bounds to the linguist radio operators who worked downstairs, and it was known as the SRTS (Short Range Technical Service) room. Even this acronym was supposedly secret as Mike Prada tells:

118

A senior officer reprimanded me on the phone for blurting out this apparently secret name after he had directed me to go to the 'upstairs' room in such a roundabout way that I felt like an idiot, because the initials were actually pinned on the door. He was obviously avoiding using them himself in the possibility that the line was tapped (we had been told that during monsoons it was easy to listen to crossed lines due to the effect of moisture). I hastily dropped the phone before he asked my name, rank and number.

This upstairs floor eventually accommodated Wireless Operators as well, because by 1959 David Iliff (No. 7 Course) remembers that a small Morse set room for their use had been added. Up to the midsummer of 1957 linguists from No. 1 Course all remember that only one W/Op came on watch with them up to Batty's, but as the upper floor was built after their departure perhaps more W/Ops were fitted in later on.

In terms of service duties and 'need to know' practice, it is clear that even the Chinese-speaking RAF officers knew little more than conscripted 'erks' about the analysis and content of their labours at Batty's. Flt Lt Paddy Raine's comment to the authors, as officer in charge at Batty's in the mid-1950s, was that officers like airmen were given a job to do and just got on with it. Perhaps as time went on it was felt appropriate for servicemen to understand a little more about the value of their work. Kenneth Wilson of No. 11 Course missed a shift after a wild night out with rugger friends,[5] and on his next shift expected to be formally reprimanded, but instead was taken 'upstairs' where the officer in charge, in strict confidence, showed him maps of the locations of Chinese radar stations and explained the crucial importance of the work in which the station was involved. On some of the later courses one of the linguists was detailed to work 'upstairs' and wore a red badge to confirm his admission to this eyrie. The services must have been constantly aware of the conflict between taking junior linguists into confidence as a means of winning total commitment to the task, and the risk of off-duty 'loose talk'; by and large, the RAF took the view, probably fully justified, that National Servicemen should know as little as possible about the processes of 'Intelligence'.

There were at least two types of high frequency radios in use during the 1950s. One was the AR88 – remembered by many and still the focus of interest of a web-based AR88 fan club – and the other the 1475, both American models. Situated at intervals along the benches, they had the standard log pads on the table beside them, and some reel-to-reel tape recorders (tapped memories recall them as Grundigs) ready at hand. These were available for those occasions when extended plain language communications were picked up by one of the scanning operators. In this case the National Service linguists would be hard pressed to write down at speed a translation of what they heard so they jumped to record it on tape, and later the Chinese native speakers would be able to play it back and clarify the messages. Reg Hunt (No. 1 Course) remembers one such incident when someone on his night watch locked onto a 'mayday' call, and this was immediately recorded on the nearest tape recorder while everyone crowded around. The emergency transmission lasted less than a minute and then stopped, and afterwards none of the linguists on that watch ever heard anymore about it or any explanation of what had happened.

On very rare occasions, a little more of the story of overheard messages could be pieced together. Mike Grindley, of No. 3 Course, was on watch when the early hours of the morning were spent following, or trying to follow, transmissions from mainland Chinese airfields tracking the path of a Nationalist plane overflying the Communist mainland. Communist planes had endeavoured to intercept it, without success, until it eventually flew out over the South China Sea. As Mike's shift was, after being relieved at 7 am, making its way by gharry down the Peak road, they saw a mysterious black-painted plane, presumably now short of fuel, landing at Kai Tak. That this was the aircraft which had been the focus of their attention for much of the night was confirmed by an article in the *South China Morning Post* of 8 April 1958, describing the plane as a four-engined P4Y military plane of the naval type, and the ten crew members were detained as 'conditional immigrants' by the Hong Kong authorities. According to the crew the plane had developed engine trouble while on a ' routine flight' and was compelled to make an emergency landing at Kai Tak. Subsequent rumour had it that the plane was dismantled and, after the fuss had died down, returned to its base in Taiwan, shipped in crates labelled 'Agricultural Parts'.

It was common knowledge among the radio operators that overflying of the mainland was a regular occurrence, whether it was designed as a spying excursion or as an exercise to test out the accuracy of the Chinese response. This conclusion was reinforced by the same article in the *South China Morning Post*, which also mentioned a Reuters report that another Chinese Nationalist Air Force plane, a F-86 Sabrejet, had been forced to land in Hong Kong on 31 January 1956; it added that the pilot was repatriated to Formosa seven weeks later, but no information was forthcoming on the fate of the aircraft itself. On a later occasion, a member of No. 5 Course tracked a plane all the way across South China into Tibet, and from a conversation with an academic colleague in the USA many years later, was able to surmise that this was a CIA leaflet-dropping operation.

The daily routine was however unexciting. At the start of each watch, the linguists sat in front of their radios, headsets at the ready, and were each given certain radio frequencies to monitor with the expected call signs – and with clear instructions not to wander onto radio broadcasts outside their brief such as Radio Hong Kong, Radio Jakarta, Radio Peking, Voice of America, AFN (American Forces Network), and so on. There was an implicit message that anyone found succumbing to this temptation would be subject to some form of sanction although there is no record of any linguist receiving severe punishment, and some even admit to the crime of light reading during the depths of the night watch. But in the normal routine, everything heard on the operator's allotted wavelengths had to be written down on the message pads; when things were quiet they wrote NHR (Nothing Heard Required). All of the voice interception work usually came in short bursts and this meant long periods of monotonous searching during the rest of the eight hour shift, which could easily translate into boredom. After being in Hong Kong for only three weeks, James McMullen (No. 5 Course) noted in his diary that the watches seemed to pass quickly, but by the end of his tour he was less enthusiastic, conceding that duty at Batty's Belvedere often occasioned nothing but boredom and frustration.

The watch officer came round frequently to check the output of each operator and would give additional wavelengths to cover if one band was apparently inactive. Specific frequencies were active at certain times of the day especially in the early morning, as regular transmissions, such as weather forecasts, came through from the airfields in Guangdong and other southern provinces. Whatever material the linguists managed to record while on duty, at the end of the eight hour shift it was the responsibility of the watch officer to collect all their log sheets, and either he or the senior man on the watch would dutifully carry this intelligence package back to Little Sai Wan, where he would pass it on to the duty officer in the Technical Block (described in chapter 2).

Many linguists remember that the transmissions were frequently a long series of numbers which had to be noted on the pads. Some sequences were in a fixed pattern that represented radar plots, and these could include reference to tracking military planes, both mainland aircraft and those coming from outside China, and also commercial flights into and out of Kai Tak (there were minimal CAAC civil flights within the mainland at that time).[6] Recording this numerical information demanded concentration on the part of the linguists, as page after page was filled with lists of numbers. Additional interest was periodically provided when , for their own reasons, the Chinese side changed the grid – this always generated a little excitement, with some justifiable satisfaction, when the operator could tell the watch officer that he had already worked out the new grid. Despite these occasions, linguists often had little or no idea about what their writings meant. They were merely gatherers of raw intelligence at the 'radio face', where, whatever more sophisticated skill in the language had been acquired, it became clear that their exhaustive training in Britain in listening to Chinese numbers had fully prepared them for carrying out this mechanical but intensive simultaneous transcription of figures.

Occasionally the Chinese radio operator's voice became recognisable. Several ex-linguists recall one in particular who, over a period of several years, was referred to as 'the Woman' or 'Yowling Annie' because of the high-pitched drone of the voice. Over time it became apparent that the voice was male, but the name stuck because, in typical military radio style, most transmissions began by testing with the routine (in Chinese) '1-2-3-4-5<>5-4-3-2-1', and the romanisation of the words 'one-two' is 'iau-leang' – which promptly becomes the deprecatory 'yowling'. By way of explanation: in G.R. the standard Chinese syllables for the numbers one and two are 'i' and 'erl'. Both of these sounds have virtually no initial consonant and they can be easily confused with seven ('chi') and ten ('shyr'), so in radio communication, in order to avoid any possible mistakes in transmission, they are changed to 'iau' and 'leang'.

In addition, all air to ground activity had to be recorded as pilots would routinely report on taking off and landing, give information on their air movements and other specialist terminology, all of which vocabulary had been included in the linguists' training programme. There were also streams of four-figure blocs of numbers that appeared regularly on the operators' logpads, the function and significance of which the linguists knew nothing, but in hindsight it is presumed that these were from the Standard Telegraphic Code (STC).[7] In the STC each four-digit bloc represents a Chinese character, and this was one method that had been used in China, way back before the foundation of the People's Republic in 1949, for transmitting written messages by telegraph and radio telephony. It is clear that the accuracy of the linguists' listening skills was paramount, as one incorrect number in a four-figure bloc could change the intended character and possibly affect the original message; or worse still, it could completely alter the meaning. No ex-linguists have reported being reprimanded for any such errors on watch, so not having the slightest idea of what was going on above their heads, the unaware and uninformed linguists could happily carry out their duties with a clear conscience.

However, the routine work could at times become quite drab, particularly when the occasional bout of resentment of conscripted service set in. Reg Hunt still has a copy of a formal note addressed to the three linguist members of his watch by their NCO, a regular serviceman, who complains that he has 'noticed a marked lack of effort from new operators which to my mind can best be described as apathetic. ... wandering around the set room is NOT part of your job, nor is sitting at the set with your headphones off. It appears that little or no effort is being put into the job in hand, the attitude of the majority being of a "couldn't care less" nature.' This short note probably sums up some of the attitudes of National Service linguists to their job although most tried to carry out their watch duties reasonably conscientiously. Minor amusements helped to pass the time on shift; occasional cryptic entries appeared in the daily diary from airmen named Cy Non and Nat Serv – when Mike Wallace was revealed to be the author of the latter he was put on a charge!

Whilst there are no records of any major disciplinary upsets at Batty's involving Chinese linguists, there had been over the years a few episodes of worker protest back at Little Sai Wan, mainly on the part of Wireless Operators, all of whom would suddenly suffer from an attack of 'deafness'. Between 1952 and 1954 three such incidents are recorded: as a protest against the differential treatment between Australian and British servicemen, as a complaint about the quality of food, or as a reaction against an order to clean the toilets after coming off night shift.[8] There was one security incident recorded at Little Sai Wan in August 1957, when an SAC (Senior Aircraftman) in one of the technical units was charged with disclosing information contrary to section 60 of the *Air Force Act*. Apparently he had written a letter, addressed but not posted to his cousin, giving details of work done by him at No. 367 SU detachment, Batty's Belvedere. He was found guilty and sentenced to 28 days' detention.[9]

A very few linguists worked in Hong Kong at other sites, not on the Peak but in the New Territories, during the 1950s. Mick Rice, a regular non-commissioned officer who studied on the first SOAS course in 1951-2, put his name forward for the single linguist position at Kong Wei:

> In mid-1954 I volunteered for a three-month detachment to Kong Wei (I was not the first linguist to man the post!). During the detachment I lived with the W/Ops, also employed there in Nissen huts on Sek Kong Airfield. The airfield was some two or three miles from Kong Wei and we were transported to and from watch in a 'clapped-out' van. The linguist and a W/Op worked together on the D/F [direction finding] equipment. The accommodation at Sek Kong was very basic compared to Little Sai Wan and the toilet facilities were positively primitive, but the meals were consistently very good and the morale on the station was splendid. I enjoyed the detachment so much that I volunteered to complete six months there.

A very small number of National Service linguists from later courses were posted in this way. Tai Mo Shan, the highest point in the New Territories, had been the home of a Japanese Direction Finding (D/F) station prior to 1945, and besides providing the radar cover for Kai Tak, the station there included an RAF radio intercept unit at the time of No. 7 Course, with staff from Batty's being occasionally sent there for a few days' duty. In 1962, Keith Drury was one of six linguists posted there – three from No. 11 Course, two from No. 10 Course, and a regular airman, together with a couple of men who had done the language course but failed the final examinations. With such small numbers, the pattern of working was quite different from that at Batty's Belvedere. There were just four men on each shift, two linguists and two radar operators, working 24 hours on and 72 hours off ('Not quite as exhausting as it sounds, as the 24-hour shift officially included meal breaks and five hours' sleep').

By arranging to swap shifts so as to complete a nominal 48-hour duty, a canny individual was then entitled to six consecutive days off. The airmen there were still however subject to extremes of weather: Keith describes one shift when a lightning storm struck one of the aerials and the bolt travelled down the aerial and across the floor where the men had their feet on the metal crossbar of the work tables, leaving a massive scorch mark on the opposite wall but the men unharmed! The RAF base on Tai Mo Shan continued in use after National Servicemen left, whilst the peak itself attracted walkers and sightseers – nowadays Hong Kong residents make a pilgrimage to the summit around the time of the New Year, because it is the only place where they are likely to see frost.

Unfortunately there are no reliable and independent figures available for the extent of work carried out at Batty's Belvedere, as distinct from Little Sai Wan. Some idea of the total activity can be gleaned from RAF files now in the National Archives. Although in August 1954 there were 15 radio sets recorded in use at Batty's,[10] records of radio intercept work appear to include the grand total of the 367 Signals Unit output, which consisted of wireless operations at Little Sai Wan and Batty's Belvedere as well as the other smaller communications outposts. For instance, in that same month, a total of 30,315 messages were intercepted, using 38 radio sets; in December 1955 this had increased to 43,782 messages intercepted using 48 sets,[11] and by January 1956 a total of 48,298 intercepts on 50 sets.[12] In October 1956, the arrival of No. 1 Course, the first of the RAF-trained National Service linguists, bright-eyed and raring to go, seems to have had little effect on the monthly output, with figures of 53 sets operating an average of 5038 set hours per week, giving a total of 49,804 messages intercepted almost the same output as in the previous January![13] A discernible rise in productivity did not occur until March 1957 when 64 radio sets with an average of 7003 set hours per week achieved a total of 61,149 message interceptions;[14] but again, it is impossible to tell what proportion of this activity arose from the work of the groups on top of the Peak.

Despite the fact that a full breakdown of ranks and trades is not feasible, it is possible to give some idea of the total manpower involved in or supporting this signals intelligence work. According to the Operations Record Book for that month,[15] on 31 January 1956 the strength of Little Sai Wan consisted of 363 RAF airmen with 18 officers, plus 16 RAAF men with their two officers, the remainder comprising one Medical Officer, one Chaplain, 13 radio fitters, 32 men from 743 Signals Unit, eight motor transport personnel, and one member from each, rank not known, of the British Army and the Australian Army. And as proof of the strategic significance of this small station and its intelligence work there were a stream of high-ranking 'scrambled egg' visitors passing through the gates. For example, in that month the 'Distinguished Visitors' included Air Chief Marshal Sir Dermot Boyle and Mr A.V.M. McDonald from the Air Ministry, many serving officers from various stations, and curiously, the Reverend E.A. Payne, General Secretary of the Baptist Union of Great Britain.

It is as well to remember that the RAF did have concern for the pastoral life and interests of their charges, and the Chaplain, Sports Officer and Education Officer were key figures in this area, so a lot of things were taking place in camp outside of duty hours. There was a cinema, library, Radio Little Sai Wan, a camp magazine called Ariel, recreation rooms, and all the usual educational courses and sports activities. Max Dolby, of No. 1 Course, offered to read short stories on the Camp Radio and was immediately accepted. He recalls venturing into a small boxroom, within the recesses of the SHQ building, that had a mike and some basic equipment for playing records, and for his fifteen-minute slots he would sit there on his own, reading humorous extracts from Thorne Smith, James Thurber and others. Because he used a radio name he got virtually no feedback on his efforts to enliven the camp's daily life, except for odd snatches of conversation overheard en passant or in the mess.

The Operations Record Book for January 1956 had two sections called 'Welfare & Education' and 'Recreation & Sport' that summarised off-duty activities. These included courses for candidates preparing for the RAF Education Tests I and II, while preparatory classes for GCE English, French, Maths and Geography for December 1956 exams were up and running. Four airmen were given resettlement interviews, fifteen books had been added to the unit library, and on the sporting side, three airmen from Little Sai Wan were runners-up in the Colony Boxing Championships. On the highbrow side, Keith Scott recalls that during his eight month tour (1956-57) there were several visiting lecturers at Little Sai Wan, including two from the University of Hong Kong, and he attended one of these talks which was given by the poet Edmund Blunden, then Professor of English at the university:

> He had a shock of white hair into which he would push his glasses while talking, and then would have to search for them whenever he wished to read something from a book. I did not know at that time that he was considered one of the leading lights of the World War I poetry movement. He later became Professor of Poetry at Oxford University.

However the days of the RAF being in control were numbered, and by March 1959 the process of the civilianisation of Little Sai Wan could be clearly seen.[16] In that month the total RAF strength was 389, including six aircrew, plus 32 Royal Australian Air Force members, but with 34 Asian civilians and 70 British civilians. As time passed details of radio operations became simplified and less informative, to the extent that in March 1961 'a total of 70 positions were manned providing an average cover of 5,371 hours per week',[17] with no mention of total messages intercepted. By that time the number of British civilians had shot up from 70 to 222 but with still the same number of 34 Asian civilians on the strength of the camp. The phasing out of the RAF presence was almost completed by September 1962 when the Operations Record Book was the last to be signed by an RAF officer, Wing Commander A.P. Morgan.[18] The following month the book was signed by a civilian as 'Head of Establishment, 367 Signals Unit', with just one RAF officer remaining on the strength; Australia, however, was still well represented with 48 RAAF personnel.

Notes

1   See Appendix B for a potted history of the origins of Batty's Belvedere by Kenneth Wilson (No. 11 Course).

2   Mike Prada records that some of No. 6 Course socialised quite a lot with the Chinese operators .

3   Apocryphal stories suggest that in the early sixties a Chinese native operator was accused of espionage by the British authorities and repatriated to mainland China.

4   David Iliff (No. 7 Course), who signed on for three years, confirms this was so when he was there in 1959-61.

5   Kenneth Wilson actually played for RAF Hong Kong in the Hong Kong Sevens, which today is one of the internationally acclaimed rugby competitions.

6   The Civil Aviation Administration of China (CAAC) was the original name of China's national airline (now named Air China), and in the 1950s there were regular internal flights taking place around the country, using mainly Soviet-built airliners. In the south of China, destinations from Guangzhou included Changsha, Haikou, Hangzhou, Nanchang, Nanning and Shanghai. Information from a CAAC Schedules Tariff booklet dated 01 October 1957, obtained by Mike Grindley (No. 3 Course) during his stay in Hong Kong.

7   A Chinese Telegraphic Code book (CTC) was compiled by Europeans in the late nineteenth century in order to transmit Chinese characters by telegraph using hand-key operators. By 1911 there were approximately 10,000 characters arranged in the traditional radical order of a dictionary, and each character was given a four-digit code number. Then

in the 1950s the People's Republic started simplifying characters and produced the new Standard Telegraphic Code book (STC) which had up to 9,000 characters in it. For more information see *en.wikipedia.org/wiki/Chinese_ Telegraphic_Code.*

8   367/6.23 and 7.61 (see Bibliography).

9   AIR 28/1331 (Little Sai Wan Operations Record Book, July 1956 to December 1959).

10   AIR 29/2284 (No. 367 SU, August 1954 to December 1955).

11   AIR 29/2284.

12   AIR 29/3764 (No. 367 SU, Little Sai Wan, 1956-1963). The final years of this file cover the initial period of civilianisation at Little Sai Wan, about which some negative publicity surfaced in later decades. The cover is stamped 'COPY – Original Destroyed due to Asbestos Contamination'.

13   AIR 29/3764.

14   AIR 29/3764.

15   AIR 29/3764.

16   AIR 29/3764.

17   AIR 29/3764.

18   AIR 29/3764.

12

NOT ALL WORK

*'At one moment to draw the bowstring tight, and at another
to release it, that is the right way to proceed in both civilian
and military life.'*

(Li Ji [Record of Rituals], an early Confucian text, 21.22)

Because of the long commute between Batty's Belvedere and Little
Sai Wan, what was nominally an eight hour watch often became an
eleven hour stint. On this basis linguists had quite generous time off.
The watch rota was based on the standard of three shifts to cover
each twenty-four hours, but its pattern was of two mornings, two
afternoons, two days off, two nights, two days off – thus actual duty
consisted of six shifts in ten days. The exact times may have varied
slightly – on the arrival of No. 3 Course Mike Grindley recorded the
times as 7 a.m. to 2.30 p.m., 2.30 to 10.15 p.m., and 10.15 p.m. to 7
a.m. – but the rota was consistent throughout our period. Since this
system, making no allowance for annual leave, requires five groups
of shift workers, the groups of National Servicemen on watch were
clearly very small, though there were usually one or two corporals
who also did intercept work, and the numbers on each watch were
bulked up by a similar handful of Chinese civilians. These erratic
hours did not suit everybody – the morning call for early watch was at
5 a.m. – but the airmen were not normally required to return to their

billets if off duty, and it was easy to take a spare shirt and trousers, change out of uniform at the end of the shift, and get dropped off the transport in Victoria Central or elsewhere along the route. For a late return to base taxis were plentiful and cheap, and as described by Mike Grindley who was on No. 3 Course, it was possible to bargain a price with taxi drivers, who fiddled their meters anyway. Besides, for a very modest charge one could stay overnight at the YMCA in Salisbury Road, near the Kowloon terminal of the Star Ferry, or at the SSAFA (Soldiers', Sailors' and Airmen's Families Association) club, or at another cheap hostelry, the China Fleet Club, so extending absence from the billet if not on duty the next day. (The worst shift was when a night watch ended on the morning of the weekly pay parade, as occasionally happened, so that the weary airmen had to stay awake and queue to sign for their pay.)

During non-working days, particularly at first, a great deal of time off was spent simply wandering the streets and markets, staring at these strange folk with exotic manners and curious tastes in food. Open-fronted streetside shops displayed dozens of plucked chickens with head attached, on hooks, or strings of fly-blown sausages, or trays of oddly shaped unaccustomed fruits. One correspondent recalls discovering fresh lychees on sale from baskets on the pavement, and trying to identify the taste which was not discovered in England until maybe thirty years later. More durable consumer goods were also plentiful, comparatively cheap, and of astonishing quality to eyes accustomed to British austerity. Many servicemen came home with a bit of China as souvenir – a silk gown for a loved one, a mah jong set, a painted or embroidered wall hanging, an ivory (or bone) carving of a horse or dragon, a cloisonné brooch or cigarette case (nearly everybody smoked at least occasionally, and tobacco was cheap). Other major purchases for servicemen were of duty-free goods often from Japan, especially cameras or wristwatches, and of tailor-made clothing, particularly shirts – for which one could be measured up one day and return to collect the made-to-measure garment on the next day. Bargaining with shopkeepers began to feel less uncomfortable, as one learnt to be a bit more assertive about it;

but the buyer still had to take care – Ken May, for instance, bought a wrapped shirt which on unpacking turned out to have no back. Given the average age of National Servicemen, there was more than one who set about buying himself a 21st birthday present; Geoff Russell's self-winding Tissot was still in use over half a century later.

Of course eating out – as a relief from RAF canteen food, and when one could afford it – was another novel experience. Many servicemen came back from Hong Kong in the 1950s with a better understanding of Chinese food – and a more expert use of chopsticks – than most folk who send out for a takeaway today. The most exotic Chinese delicacies were available, and a spirit of gastronomic adventure helped, although bird's nest soup and hundred-year-old eggs were outside the financial scope of most. Also near the limits of National Servicemen's income, but something most airmen had to do at least once, was to take 'Tea at the Pen'. The Peninsula Hotel in Kowloon was – and still is – the most prestigious hotel-restaurant in the colony, and the smartest set of ex-pats would resort there for afternoon tea: a proper English tea with cucumber sandwiches and pastries, and a 'Palm Court' group of musicians on a hidden balcony playing popular melodies. Well-to-do Chinese families would also partake, and were observed to have no reticence in shouting 'Boy!' for an elderly waiter to replenish the teapot – a condescension no Westerner would have got away with. With a little trepidation, and after having checked the wallet, a serviceman dressed in civvies could on a rare occasion enjoy there the kind of uniformed waiter service that few would have aspired to in the 1950s back home. Elsewhere linguists were advised to be on their guard, as it was rumoured that in some less prestigious establishments the bar girls were Communist agents and were particularly interested in the activities of servicemen from Little Sai Wan.

On a more proletarian note, Bill Mellows recalls that the first time he ever saw a club sandwich was during his tour of duty around 1958, such extravagance being still rare in Britain. Several men remember discovering the ice cream dish Baked Alaska in Hong

Kong – doubtless an American influence – and Ken Brooks was not alone in enjoying San Miguel beer, the typical tipple in the colony. One place known to many linguists for a relaxing 'San Mig' was Jack Condor's Bar, tucked away in the Central area. There was a western-style atmosphere inside, without any hostesses on duty as in the Wanchai bars, and it catered mainly to a 'Gwai Lo' male clientele. Suffice it to say that No. 1 Course chose this neutral ground for its 'End of tour' party in April 1957, before imminent repatriation to Blighty from May onwards.

At the same time as enjoying these luxuries, most men were aware of the poverty and degradation that surrounded the comfortable colonial life, and were saddened by the crippled, the beggars and the destitute who could not be avoided in the streets. The makeshift shanty towns on the hillsides of the island and of Kowloon were visible to everyone in Hong Kong, and with the influx of refugees from across the frontier at that time meaning an increase in population of up to 50% year on year, the future of the colony seemed sometimes to be in more peril than the future of the Cold War world. Prostitution was common; servicemen came to understand the emphasis placed on the avoidance of venereal diseases in films that they had been forced to watch in basic training, and which had seemed at the time rather comic entertainments; and of course some airmen indulged. British servicemen became aware, too, that there seemed to be more girls on the streets of Wanchai when the US Navy was in harbour. Besides, many young women, rather more honestly, sought out servicemen in a desperate attempt to engage in a serious relationship with the possibility of escape from poverty in the colony. Such contacts were not easy, because a serviceman obviously could not take a woman back to his barracks, and less affluent Chinese would be unwilling to invite a European to their unsophisticated home for fear of losing face. Mike Prada tells a story about himself and a friend being invited – most unusually – to the shack of a girl they had met, where she got out the best cups but had only weak green tea to offer. Over the years, there were rumours about various airmen moving in with local women, but inter-racial marriages were severely frowned on by all the Services, and were very rare. There were stories about individuals being promptly shipped home if an affair promising to become serious came to the attention of senior officers.

Readers might reasonably assume that linguists were more able to fraternise with native Chinese, or at least to have through conversation a better understanding of local issues and perceptions, but in fact the vast majority of Hong Kong residents are Cantonese speaking, and although they in general use the same written characters, Cantonese is not so much a dialect of standard Mandarin as a separate language with its own colloquial vocabulary and tonal system. Serious conversation in Mandarin Chinese was therefore only possible with the better educated, who of necessity in the colony usually spoke good English and preferred to practise it. But there were always stories of linguists finding Mandarin-speaking staff in the Wanchai bars, and being able to develope their spoken language in such situations at leisure, with alcohol often proving a valuable stimulant towards producing a more fluent flow of Chinese from their lips.

When urban life began to pall it was possible to explore about twenty miles inland into the New Territories, as far as Sheung Shui which was the last legally accessible station, for British personnel, on the Kowloon-Canton railway line. Any attempt by a serviceman to approach the actual border was of course strictly forbidden. Similarly out of bounds was the notorious Queen's Road East in Wanchai, an area whose bars and brothels meant that a naïve European could be at risk of robbery or contagious disease, and being found there by a Military Police patrol would lead to a severe reprimand. Other forbidden areas in the city, for political reasons as well as those of personal safety, were the densely populated area of Mong Kok and the administratively anomalous Kowloon Walled City, which was nominally within the jurisdiction of the government in Beijing.

Within these limitations, exploration of the villages and bathing beaches was easy. Taking the short train or bus trip from Kowloon

135

into the hinterland, away from the assumed protection of the city, was itself an adventure. 'Off the roads of the New Territories, the picture-hungry will find cameos of the real China beyond' – claimed the Far East Transport Wing 'Route Guide', a copy of which was issued to air passengers coming into the colony – 'the China of crazy roll-picture hills, of padi landscapes and toiling peace, of labour and life incessant' (who thought the RAF lacked imagination?). John Henty describes going by train, in civvies of course, to the last permitted station on the edge of the Closed Region, and on another occasion taking a ferry round Tolo Harbour, the boat docking at all the outlying villages to load or unload livestock. Back on the island, a jaunt to Repulse Bay was a favourite because it had the Repulse Bay Hotel, now sadly disappeared, where one could have an afternoon tea experience a little more cheaply than at the 'Pen'. Rather closer to base, Big Wave Bay and Sheko on the east side of Hong Kong island – although then, unlike today, totally unexploited for tourism – provided safe bathing; while Aberdeen on the south coast had a reputation for its floating restaurants where one could choose one's own live fish from tanks, to have them immediately cooked. And there was swimming off the rocks immediately outside the barracks of Little Sai Wan itself. Going into town, there were always the clanking trams – Ken Brooks mentions his favourite tram journey, all the way from Kennedy Town to Shaukiwan – and the Star Ferry, costing 10 cents on the lower deck and 20 cents on the upper deck (at the rate of 100 cents to the Hong Kong dollar, which itself exchanged for 1s 3d, or just over six pence in today's coin). One of the attractions of the tram journey for Ken and others was that it enabled them to revise their knowledge of written characters by reading the shop signs!

Inevitably the behaviour of some servicemen was at times out of order. Mike Grindley (No. 3 Course) reports how he was one of three linguists relaxing in a Lockhart Road bar when a couple of sailors drunkenly tried to smash the place up. The culprits were later taken before a local magistrate – in the event they pleaded guilty, so Mike and friends were not required to give evidence. However the young and inexperienced examining magistrate turned out to be a certain Tony Leathlean, who already had a legal qualification when he served on No. 1 Course! He eventually was made a High Court judge in Hong Kong.

Apart from the tourist activities of shopping and sightseeing, and generally seeking the sybaritic life, many linguists sought another kind of escape from the barracks by trying to integrate, however briefly, into the colony's social activities. This was not always easy, partly because of the temporary nature of most servicemen's stay, but also because of the conscripts' awareness that ex-pat colonials for the most part led a sheltered life away from the sordid bustle of the city. For instance Mike Grindley and three friends off watch attended the local Catholic church and were taken home to dinner by a church member, to share a nine-course meal that included carp and tortoise. Of course many civilians stood aloof from military personnel, but others displayed unrequited generosity, whether they were European or Chinese. As far as the linguists were concerned, the majority had university or professional training or similar expectations, so saw themselves, rightly or wrongly, as being more ambitious and more cosmopolitan than the average serviceman, and a considerable number became involved in non-service activities within the colony. James McMullen made friends at the Anglican Cathedral, where John Norrish had earlier sung in the choir, which consisted of Chinese and Europeans in approximately equal numbers. John also joined a group called the Hong Kong Singers, conducted by a professor from the university – he recalls a 'surreal' evening singing 'Merrie England' halfway up the Peak 'to a group of colonials who were dressed as colonials', and wondering if he looked like them. Geoff Russell joined the Hong Kong Stage Club, which put on half a dozen theatrical performances in the year. At least one adventurous group went to see live Chinese opera, and were startled and fascinated by the way that the opera was treated as a sort of massive cabaret, with many in the audience eating, chatting, or coming and going throughout the four or five hour performance. Others, including some from John Henty's group, visited the leper colony on Hay Ling island on a trip organised by Thea Yandle, 'a delightful WRVS [Women's Royal Voluntary Service] lady', while Keith Drury of No. 11 Course enterprisingly volunteered to work there for a week during his leave. Mike Wallace (No. 7 Course) joined a drama group called the Garrison Players and played hockey for RAF Hong Kong, while Kenneth Wilson, also of No. 11 Course, found himself refereeing soccer in Hong Kong League matches. Ken Glover of No. 1 Course played cricket for the RAF on their gloriously situated home ground at Kai Tak, whilst his course colleague Terry Keyms played rugby for RAF Hong Kong, usually on less comfortable pitches dried as hard as concrete, against tough sailors just arrived in port. Other men took part over the years in a variety of sports, both inter-services and civilian teams.

However, whilst the single young men with no other responsibilities could lead this kind of carefree life, it was not quite so easy for some of the slightly older men – particularly in the later years of National Service – who might already have a wife, dependants, or property back home. Mike Greenall of No. 9 Course, already a graduate and married three weeks before call-up, found that others like him had so little spending money after the deduction of marriage allowance and compulsory savings that they had to moonlight, to earn income additional to their service duties. He himself taught English, first to the Chinese wives of English officers and later through advertising in a local paper, earning HK$10 per hour to supplement his RAF pay. He remembered another man who was on the rota for night duty but told the officer in charge that he was unable to do that shift because he had a job as 'Night Owl' for Radio Hong Kong! There was some envy of the Australians at Little Sai Wan, who were seen as doing the same work but were paid more – as were the civilian operators who began to take over the duties of linguists. Nevertheless Mike felt that life in Little Sai Wan was like that of a holiday camp, where the typical off-duty dress – at least in summer – was shorts, flip-flops and a towel, maybe topped with an RAF beret.

With so much novelty, so much to see and hear and do, it is perhaps not surprising that what most members of the linguist groups remember about this period in their lives is of what they did off-duty, rather than of what went on inside Batty's Belvedere. In that respect, although they had all signed the Official Secrets Act in deadly earnest, and in general took their wireless duties quite seriously, there was little risk of a breach of security – life away from Batty's was far too interesting!

Once settled into the barracks at Hong Kong and the working routine of Batty's Belvedere, many men throughout the National Service groups could not resist the urge to try to explore more widely in the Far East. Travel into mainland China was of course impossible in those Maoist years, when migration even for the Chinese was difficult, whilst for the Europeans this outpost of Empire was felt to be a haven on the very edge of hostile territory. Some men did however find ways of travelling further afield, mainly towards the south.

John Henty attended the station chapel in Little Sai Wan. 'One day the padre mentioned that a week's moral leadership course was being held in Singapore… It was amazing how attendance at Sunday morning service suddenly shot up. But… the padre was having none of this' and just four regular churchgoers were offered the trip. 'We arrived at Changi airport to find a red carpet laid out and a welcoming reception, which we duly acknowledged as we left the plane. After all, we were important Chinese linguists and this was nothing less than we deserved. It seems that we had been travelling with some local dignitary, and were quickly bundled out of the way!' Nevertheless the four had a great time: the course was held on the island of Blakang Mati (the 'Island of Death', where there was once a Royal Artillery barracks – since then the old barracks have been transformed into a holiday centre linked to Singapore by cable car, the island being renamed Sentosa, Malay for 'tranquillity'!),[1] and they 'explored the remains of the World War II fortifications… where the guns famously pointed the wrong way', swam nude on one of the isolated beaches, and took tea at the Raffles Hotel.

Closer to base was the (then) 90-minute boat trip to Lan Tao Island – now the site of Chek Lap Kok International Airport, but in the 1950s still a land of paddy fields, rocky footpaths, and silence. Thus it was a retreat, as recorded in Geoff Russell's diary, for him and three others to avoid the incessant racket of Chinese New Year in Hong Kong. One of just two places to stay – the other was a Trappist monastery – was at the Buddhist monastery, Po Lin, an hour's walk from the little ferry jetty, across rice fields, into the hills. There the intrepid visitors were met by a shaven monk in brown robe, and offered lodging in a bare wooden room with slatted beds, directly above the temple where morning devotions with gongs and chanting began at 4.30 a.m. The next day the visiting quartet was taken across more hills to see the equivalent women's establishment, where female followers of the Buddha also wore the brown robe with shaven head, so that the sexes were practically indistinguishable. The hospitality was generous and the food on offer was vegetarian, simple but ample. No payment was ever requested, and Geoff for long afterwards felt the voluntary contribution made, albeit from a serviceman's limited pay, was too mean!

The nearest 'foreign' country which was relatively easy to visit, and required no passport, was the Portuguese possession of Macao. Although colonised in the 16th century – the first European settlement in the Far East – and for two hundred years a distant source of conflict between Portugal, Spain and Holland, with a sizeable minority population of Roman Catholics, the peninsula was never exploited like Hong Kong, where the natural harbour was deeper. Consequently Macao had become a rather sleepy, slightly louche place, where European expatriates and the better-off Chinese went for pleasure. With its mixture of faded Mediterranean-colonial villas and Buddhist temples within crowded streets and green parks, it had the laid-back reputation of being home to gaming houses and prostitutes. Keith Drury in 1962 booked into the Central Hotel with three mates from Batty's, who on arrival were met at the end of the corridor by a Chinese man with four young women -'You want company?' The other preoccupation, with gambling, has continued, and since 2004 Macao's casino income has exceeded that of Las Vegas.[2]

For most National Servicemen, this was the limit of exploration. However, within the fairly generous limits of leave and the occasional possibility of swapping work shifts, the more adventurous in due course discovered ways to travel much farther afield without enormous expense. The secret of this was to find out about spare passenger capacity in USAF transports, known as 'indulgence flights'. RAF planes might only make regular flights to and from Singapore, but the United States military flew frequently between Hong Kong, Manila in the Philippines, and Japan (presumably also to Chinese Nationalist Taiwan, but the authors never heard of anyone going there).

Mike Prada of No. 6 Course relates an extensive trip he took with jolly company:

> I had to report… to the MATS (Military Air Transport Service) office. I had to report in uniform but quickly shed it once on board. However it was a DC3 (C47) Dakota and all the main seats were removed except four at the front. The free area contained several camphorwood chests and an upright piano. It all seemed rather overloaded to me. Obviously this had been a 'shopping trip' under the guise of a training flight. It all seemed very jovial and friendly on board with no reference to rank. All seats were occupied by other USAF personnel, including two bunks behind the pilot. My attention was drawn to a heap of parachutes at the back of the plane near the loo. Our take-off from Kai Tak seemed to be quite laboured and I prayed none of the 'cargo' would come loose.

However Mike landed in Okinawa, where at the Kadena Officers' Club, from that day's menu, you could order a 1½ lb. porterhouse steak for one dollar, including a double Manhattan! After a three-week trip visiting Tokyo, Kyoto and Nara, Mike returned from Kobe on a Dutch ferry which gave a concessionary rate for UK servicemen. Surviving a typhoon and being buzzed by an overflight of MIG-15 aircraft off the Chinese mainland, he eventually made it back to Little Sai Wan.

Mike also recalls the adventures of a fellow linguist who, after meeting an Australian girl on vacation in Hong Kong, decided to visit her in her home country. Succeeding in getting offered a place on a religious retreat to Singapore, he played hookey and found a spare seat on a military flight to Oz. After a few days (the story does not record how successful his romantic trip was), he got himself airlifted back to Singapore but then was stuck in Changi airbase because he had missed the 'official' return flight, was penniless, and depended on other charitable servicemen to take him into the NAAFI. Eventually getting back on duty after some weeks' absence, and having to attend pay parade where several weeks' money was uncollected, he got away with the explanation that he had been saving up, swapping lots of night shifts so as not to be tempted to spend his weekly pay, and allowing his pay to accumulate... Similarly, one airman was reputed to have gone off without permission to Indochina, because he wanted to see Angkor Wat.

Maybe the RAF got wise to this plan of accidentally going AWOL (absent without leave), because Ken Brooks of No. 8 Course remembered that if an airman went on any of these jaunts, he had to demonstrate sufficient funds to enable him to return by civilian transport if an indulgence flight was not available. Thus Peter Shortell, who was on No. 5 Course, got to Okinawa

> using simply [his] RAF ID card as travel document and leave card. The US forces insisted on stamping the leave card every day, but it was not very big and had no space for such stamps. It puzzled them even more than my accent!

However Peter got as far as Yokohama, Tokyo and Nikko, but also had to guarantee his own return passage by ship.

This facility for further travel seems to have been available until the end. Another adventurer, Keith Drury of No. 11 Course, hitched a lift on a US plane to Clark Field near Manila, and remembers it as the most uncomfortable journey ever taken – ' in wicker chairs strapped to the floor in what appeared to be the unheated cargo hold'.

142

However on arrival Keith and companions were asked by US airmen what was their intention whilst in Manila; since the Britishers had little cash they proposed to live cheaply, sleep in the beach environs, whatever, but the Yanks would not hear of this and insisted that they sleep in the American billets and eat in the American canteen, where the food was excellent, so their trip was a real holiday.

Notes

1   See Bright (2003), or *http://www.guardian.co.uk/travel/2003/aug/31/ singapore.observerescapesection?page=3.*

2   *en.wikipedia.org/Macao.*

13

BUDDING MERITOCRATS IN THE COLD WAR

*'Here linguists were trained for covert work, their vigilance
contributing to national security during the Cold War.'*

*(Commemorative plaque for the Joint Services School
for Linguists placed in St Thomas à Becket Church,
Pucklechurch, Bristol on 22 May 2006 by the RAF
Linguists Association)[1]*

The 1950s generation of National Service linguists were all born in
the 1930s or during the early years of World War II, and would have
absorbed the cultural imprint of the social values of those times from
parents, grandparents, friends, school and everyday life. Wartime
conditions must have had some effect on their outlook on life, with
the increased demand for social conformity and national solidarity,
and a feeling of sharing and working together towards the common
good and final victory. For example, food and clothing rationing
which had only completely ended by 1954, affirmed this apparently
level playing field for most of the population and the inevitable
black market[2] in existence then did not seem to adversely affect the
public acceptance of this forced equality brought about by the war.
Traditional values of the times did not usually offer children as many
personal rights or as much family status as today's young people
growing up in child-centred families. On the other hand, unlike the
conditions prevailing today, they had much more freedom to go out to

play in the street in safety, without too much worry for their parents. They could mix with other kids and absorb how to get on with each other, and hopefully learn something about personal responsibility as they grew up. And at the same time they had to conform to the prevailing mores of the British way of life, and 'Grin and bear it'; even if this meant more self-control and self-discipline in order to suppress that youthful individualism which might lead them to transgress the norms of society; whilst for males, the conditioning syndrome of 'Little boys don't cry' was always lurking just below the surface of everyday life.

The period 1945-73 in the UK was characterised in *British Social Trends since 1900* edited by A.H. Halsey, as being one of economic and social stability with comparatively low unemployment, and that only after the oil crisis of 1973 did things start to change. Such stable conditions in the 1950s were an ideal environment for ambitious scholarship boys going to grammar school and then finding that their educational background opened up opportunities for them to forge careers way beyond the dreams of their grandparents. But first there was the unknown hurdle of National Service facing them. Donald Sutton (No 5 Course) has given his thoughts on the reactions of linguists to the RAF:

> As a backdrop it seems to me important to note the post-imperial malaise that was settling into Britain, a rather drab place in the 1950s. We were more or less of the same generation and background as the irreverent satirists of Beyond the Fringe, and like them many of us were already admitted to university. Our position near the bottom of the totem pole fostered a certain irreverence towards authority. I'm not thinking of the generally impressive and likeable language school officers, but the more foolish of the officers encountered outside the course. We had memorably unrealistic exercises, films and lectures on 'atomic' war (which one officer rhymed with 'gnome'). We found tiresome the rituals of the weekly parade and were puzzled by the odd preamble to prayer which instructed Roman Catholics and 'members of the Jewish faith' to fall out.

National Service was an entirely new experience for every conscript. For a start they had to obey all orders from anyone with authority over them whatever their personal feelings about him. The Cold War period did have real wars taking place and one crucial response in wartime is risking one's life on the instructions of another man or facing the dire consequences of disobeying orders. For a reality check on the effects of war on men, official sources state that large numbers of servicemen due to take part in the D-Day invasion in World War II went absent without leave (AWOL). In fact the great majority of the 1950s generation of conscripts did presumably carry out their orders, and as a result National Servicemen were killed in Korea, Malaya and other theatres of war. There is no further information on the British Armed Forces website[3] as to how many National Servicemen went AWOL, but it says that 395 National Servicemen lost their lives on active service, and many more were wounded in action or injured in accidents. It is interesting to ponder whether this period could be categorised as that of the last generation of conscripted men who would go 'over the top' like in World War I and World War II, especially if there was no direct threat to the nation. Of course, this is purely 'old generation' thinking, and anyway there has been no military conscription since National Service ended in 1962. As a reflection of the linguists' times John Henty (No. 6 Course) remembers that 'we had our attitude to the country, we accepted a level of authority higher than today, but those were the rules of the game and we never complained. We had a sense of humour, group cohesion and we marched in formation everywhere'.

Along with every other conscript, on joining up the linguists had to undergo the initial RAF process of basic training to get them mentally conditioned to service life. Conscript airmen were quite a trial to the regular non-commissioned officers (NCOs) but in reality those sergeants and corporals had the full authority of RAF regulations as backup. Any airman committing a misdoing, whether accidental or intended, could suffer immediate retribution in the form of 'jankers' (punishment), which might consist of cleaning the latrines or scraping out the huge cooking vats in the kitchens, a daunting task especially after porridge had been on the breakfast menu.

It is clear to see that during square-bashing the NCOs came down hard on any personalities or characters who might upset the group discipline that they were trying to instil within the motley ranks of conscripts; the service ethic demanded all airmen must work as a disciplined team and subordinate their individuality accordingly. So with this coerced co-operation from recruits the NCOs gradually achieved some success. In return conscripts learnt to have a quick-witted and protective response when questioned by anyone in authority, and most of all they should not grin or smile as this could lead to a charge of 'dumb insolence' and consequent sanctions. However the ultimate challenge for the square-bashing NCOs was to weld all recruits, by the means of constant drill practice, into disciplined squads who could march together in vaguely co-ordinated step and eventually perform a satisfactory Passing-Out Parade before the Officer Commanding.

The old service mantra for survival that was constantly preached by the NCOs was 'bullshit baffles brains', an attitude of mind that seems to have been polished into sophisticated forms and honed in practice in many layers of society today. Keith Scott (No. 1 Course) remembers that Flying Officer Hargreaves, one time Education Officer at RAF Hednesford in the glorious summer of 1955, had an explanation for the derivation of the word 'bullshit', which he claimed was a corruption of an old Elizabethan word 'bolshon' meaning 'to clean up'. This seems to tie in well with the slang usage of 'bull', vividly expressed in erk-talk as 'brasso, blanco and bull'. However the intrinsic connotation of the 'bullshit' saying contains traces of deceiving and exploiting someone, or making mockery of them, and in this case the Old French verb 'boler' or 'bouler' (to deceive)[4] might be a better bet.

Some No. 1 Course members on starting their language studies tried to translate this mantra into Chinese with the guidance of the native-speaking tutors, but sadly in the process it lost all its idiomatic punch. The direct word-for-word translation from Chinese, in a form sometimes referred to as 'Chinglish', is 'Male-ox-excrement-confuse-intelligent-person', which is not exactly a comprehensible statement for an uninformed Chinese listener to respond to or even absorb. A salutary lesson on the translation of expressions, sayings and idioms from a European language to an Oriental one, and vice versa. Nevertheless the shrewdest airmen who practised this principle could often achieve results that were admired and envied by most of their peers. As examples, a keen musician from No. 1 Course got the RAF to pay for trumpet lessons off-camp, whilst another member, a fast bowler of repute who played at Minor Counties level, was often away from duty playing cricket for RAF Wythall, the Combined Services and RAF Hong Kong; yet a third member boxed and played rugby for RAF Hong Kong. For sheer audacity and ingenuity, David Iliff has a story about a Chinese linguist from one of the later courses who for some reason was temporarily transferred to RAF Kai Tak. Living accommodation there was in large communal billets and as a lowly Junior Technician they should have been his abode. However, he managed to persuade the powers-that-be that he sometimes talked in his sleep and so might unconsciously reveal classified information to any other inmates in the billet who maybe lacked the necessary security clearance. As a result he was given a single room usually reserved solely for NCOs. One can only wonder at his success rate in life after the RAF.

In order to be considered for language training in the Royal Air Force the minimum requirement was to have the core G.C.E.s or a professional qualification of some kind, so this meant that most linguists had been through grammar or independent school and in fact the majority were apparently from modest but aspiring segments of society. This seems to indicate that linguist trainees in addition to being reasonably well educated also had the ambition, initiative and curiosity to widen their knowledge by applying for foreign language courses. On the other hand maybe they were smart enough to recognise an interesting two-year 'skive' (the easiest option) when it presented itself. Perhaps they could be regarded as exemplars of the rise of meritocracy in post-war Britain, whereby their career prospects depended more on their abilities and academic results than on the pull of old traditional family contacts or Old School Tie networks. It is possible that RAF recruits from the more advantaged social backgrounds had already been skimmed off and selected for officer training during their basic training and this might account for the small number of linguists from such privileged backgrounds. The few boarding-schoolers seemed to mix well and they were generally adept at keeping their heads down before authority, both traits perhaps resulting from their survival course in a boarding background.

One further requirement for National Service was to pass the medical examination. Although the numbers are not known, young men were regularly exempted from National Service on various medical grounds, some of which appeared to be fairly trivial. At that time in the mid-50s the most famous case was that of M.C. Cowdrey who had a not uncommon condition known as 'flat feet', a Class III medical classification according to RAF standards. Yet despite this apparent handicap he continued to develop his cricket career and went on to successfully captain England, and later in life he became President of the MCC (Marylebone Cricket Club). In contrast, Keith Scott at his initial medical was found to have both flat feet and defective eyesight; this caused much clucking and head shaking from the Medical Officer before the young man was finally assessed as Class II medically fit, and thus became eligible for recruitment into the RAF fold. By such slim chances can one's life be changed for ever.

However no matter where they hailed from, the budding linguists had the exuberance and confidence of youth, with plenty of 'personalities' within their ranks from all parts of Britain; and they all suddenly had the great shock of adjusting to living and being together in a huge organisation that had myriad rules and regulations. John Henty (No. 6 Course) had the feeling 'of not being free, not being able to do what we wanted and not being in control of our lives. On the other hand everything was done for us and we had the time and enough money to follow our inclinations.' This was a situation in which the extremely small number of boarding school linguists had quite an advantage over the others in that they were already used to a disciplined, communal life and routine and so were easily able to make the seamless transition from boarding life to service life after the initial trauma of eight weeks' tough square-bashing. And during that basic training all the low-ranking airmen had to follow the service rules, which could be arbitrarily imposed on them by anyone of higher rank i.e. corporals or above, when logic and fair play did not always figure in the verbal exchanges. Such an environment could rankle at first and was an ideal breeding ground for 'bolshie' behaviour from young airmen, but when the linguists started their studies they gradually realised that their language course gave them some protection and privileges, with the additional attraction of a plum posting to Hong Kong at the end.

Perhaps the linguists' feelings about their lot in RAF life could be summarised as a spectrum of attitudes ranging from stoic acceptance through humorous irreverence to suppressed disaffection, incipient cynicism and traces of bolshieness (towards NCOs and authority in particular). Donald Sutton recalls:

> In Hong Kong I remember the visit of the Duke of Edinburgh when on duty in the reception flight awaiting the arrival of his aircraft at Kai Tak Airport. We stood for several hours by the runway in tropical kit, and a number of airmen fainted one after the other on the hot tarmac, and when his plane landed we watched him step down and speed by in a jeep, waving and never pausing to exchange a few words. This sort of experience did not produce resentment but only fed the sense of amused irreverence. Later I realised that the two Air Force years were a formative experience of working within a large organisation where one learned to go along with the rules. As juniors you couldn't try to reshape the organisation's rules, but had somehow to find harmony with them.

Interestingly in his diary James McMullen (No. 5 Course) also records the Duke's visit on 5 March 1959, and the great interest that this created in Hong Kong colonial society. He notes that the Duke during his stay addressed all three branches of the armed services, giving one and a half hours to the Senior Service and a mere seven minutes to the Royal Air Force! His laconic diary comment of 'Jolly good' seems to be a simple example of this irreverent attitude of National Servicemen.

Interviews with ex-RAF Chinese linguists during preparation of this book revealed a range of feelings about their National Service experience. There were many positive responses, as from John Henty (No. 6 Course): 'I have only fond and happy memories of my National Service days. We learnt a language and saw the world, and friendships were forged that have lasted almost fifty years.' Others were resigned to the inevitability of it all, but hardly anything negative came up, except for some dissatisfaction with the pay and the fact that two years of service was too long, especially for married men. A member of No. 9 Course recalls that his course of about 14 members were mainly deferred entrants, almost all graduates, so they were rather older than average and one or two were married. As he put it, when they joined up the end of National Service was in sight, and it was generally regarded as a waste of time, with a high level of resentment and frustration amongst linguists, especially about J/T pay. So much so that some of the course moonlighted in Hong Kong to make more money, and our informant himself taught English for $10HK per hour to the Chinese wives of various servicemen. This reveals quite a difference in attitude between the carefree eighteen year old trainees without any commitments, who could survive happily on the RAF wages, compared to the older maturer men who came into the service after several years deferment working for a qualification or university degree, and maybe even being married. However he ended up by saying that in retrospect National Service was the most positive time of his life and not only affected his future career but taught him discipline and self-reliance.

The most common response from ex-linguists about the overall experience was that it had widened their horizons and in some cases had provided unimagined opportunities for future careers, sometimes in or related to Chinese. One linguist from an early 1950s SOAS training course said 'National Service was a good thing for me, it completely changed my life in a positive way and Chinese studies became a part of my future career.' They had done something useful in learning a foreign language, they had travelled to the other side of the world and encountered quite a different culture, and all this had developed their maturity and outlook on life. Kenneth Wilson (No. 11 Course) felt 'that National Service was a disaster for me to start with because it interrupted my accountancy career. On reflection it taught me to do things properly and to put in more effort, and it changed my attitude for the good. But afterwards I went back to accountancy.' In terms of overseas travel most ex-linguists admitted that before National Service and going to Hong Kong they had not travelled outside of the UK.

Amongst the Chinese linguists, some of them with Sixth Form[5] backgrounds already had university places held for them after their service, while others were destined for the professions, such as accountancy, banking, business, insurance, journalism, law, religion and teaching; and a few were still thinking about what to do post-RAF. Keith Drury (No. 11 Course) said that out of the fifteen members of his group, most of whom were grammar school products, no one went on to university and five of them became bank managers. He himself was offered a civilian operator's job in Hong Kong after demob[6] but his bride-to-be demurred at the prospect of this move. It is impossible to establish with certainty how this Chinese language experience affected the lives of the trainees involved because there are no records of the subsequent careers of all the linguists. The closest estimate of the numbers that were trained on the 11 Chinese Courses organised by the RAF from September 1955 to August 1961, totals just over 250, this figure being derived entirely from the interviews and research done for this book, and it is not possible to give accurate facts or figures for all of them. Reg

Hunt (No. 1 Course) checked with the other seventeen members still in touch with each other, and he found that eight of them had gone on to university after National Service. In terms of careers they had produced one accountant, two bank managers, three businessmen, four civil servant/local government officers, four teachers and four university staff (two in Chinese studies). The middle course was No. 6, and John Henty has listed the career patterns of 23 of his group – two accountants, one bank manager, four businessmen, five civil servant/local government officers, two company secretaries, one in entertainment, one in finance, one librarian, one in insurance, one minister of religion, three teachers and one in travel.

Looking through the feedback from all the informants there appears to be some indication that a significant minority of all the linguists are thought to have been so influenced by their National Service that afterwards they continued with their Chinese, and used it in their workplace or academic institution. In academic terms the UK universities in the 1960s benefitted from the success of these RAF courses. If they had any staffing needs there was this pool of ex-Chinese speaking linguists, who were attracted by Chinese culture and studies, and eager to follow an academic career. In fact some of this cohort, now at retirement age, reached professorial level or equivalent in academia. They were ever present throughout the decades following the 1950s in Oriental Departments in UK and Commonwealth universities (and even in the US), as well as working in university libraries, museums and at GCHQ. An anecdote from James McMullen about the McMullen twins (No. 5 Course) well illustrates this point. With their A Levels of Ancient History, Greek and Latin they already had university places awaiting them to study Classics after finishing National Service:

> One afternoon my brother David and I went down on the rocks in front of Little Sai Wan to work on our classics for forthcoming university studies in England; it was Sophocles – Oedipus Tyrannus, and as we tried to translate we could see Chinese junks silently sailing by and everything suddenly seemed remote and incongruous.

Their exposure to the Chinese language, and then subsequently to the culture and way of life in Hong Kong had a life-changing effect on them, because after National Service they both pursued academic careers in Oriental Studies.

Some five decades later looking back on their National Service life, most linguists expressed the view that the RAF Chinese Language courses were extremely well taught, organised and administered, and the relationship between officer and NCO teaching staff and students, in terms of the normal context of the Armed Services, was unusually relaxed and benign. John Henty felt that 'the course was well-structured, the teaching was good both from RAF officers and NCOs, with Joe Cant being superb, and the Chinese instructors were fascinating when talking about their past.' And as for military discipline, most linguists recall little intrusion of this into their service life after square-bashing was over, unless they overstepped boundaries and went too far in their horseplay or behaviour, in which case summary justice, usually watered down by the Officer-in-Charge of the Chinese programme, would be administered. In a way the language units were protected from humdrum discipline, and the general feeling was that the linguists felt elitist and very privileged to be learning Chinese.

Then when they actually started radio voice interception work in Hong Kong after their one year's training, there was the sudden realisation that they were involved in a real military situation and this was a serious matter. There was always the threat of invasion from across the border, because Hong Kong was indefensible against the might of the People's Liberation Army (PLA), certainly in terms of pre-atomic normal land warfare. And linguists would have had no notion of whether any diplomatic threats of atomic attack on China by western powers had been communicated to the Chinese government at any time during or after the Korean War. This change from language learning in Britain to practical reality in China could also trigger some deeper consideration of what they were actually doing. For example, according to Peter Shortell

(No. 5 Course), one of their group decided to opt out of this type of work for moral reasons, viz. 'spying wasn't cricket', and he was immediately transferred to Christmas Island as a stores clerk. He later wrote to his ex-colleagues to say life was very boring there but he was saving most of his pay. At times the RAF could work very effectively when pushed.

Although the linguists knew almost nothing then about the end product of their work, it is now known that they were part of RAF Signals Intelligence (SIGINT), and that they were working in a very small component of some complicated apparatus of British intelligence gathering during the Cold War. In Chapter 2 a balanced overview of this subject has already been presented and from this one can see that the radio voice interception work in Hong Kong, which was just a very small fragment of secret RAF history, slotted in as one of the many strands of the complex web leading to GCHQ, the government organisation that had replaced Bletchley Park after World War II. It is a great honour for the small group of Chinese linguists, whose hidden National Service story is celebrated in these pages, to be associated with that famous 'Intelligence' establishment which broke the German Enigma codes in the 1940s. And today, some of those linguists look back with a degree of pride on their small contribution towards the defence of the realm in that Cold War period. At the unveiling of the Pucklechurch plaque by the Director of GCHQ, on 22 May 2006, he thanked all JSSL linguists for their work and efforts during those times. For the two of the authors present at this ceremony it was the first time in fifty years that any praise from above had been heard for the linguists' intelligence-gathering activities. A pleasing and unexpected tribute which was much appreciated.

Notes

1   *www.rafling.co.uk* The commemorative plaque was unveiled by the present Director of GCHQ.

2   Black market was the term for illegal trading in mainly rationed goods.

3   *www.britisharmedforces.org.*

4   Walter W. Skeat, *Etymological Dictionary of the English Language.* Oxford: The Clarendon Press, 1974 impression.

5   Sixth Form refers to the two senior years (16-18 years of age) at secondary school.

6   'Demob' is short for 'demobilisation', i.e. official discharge from the Armed Forces after completing term of service.

14

THE STREAM FLOWS ON

'Standing beside a stream, the Master said:
Time flows along just like this, never stopping day or
night.'
(Confucian Analects, 9.17)

As the end of the 1950s approached, it was becoming increasingly apparent that Britain's military needs and priorities were changing, and that for the foreseeable future they could best be met by maintaining smaller and more efficient armed forces, made up of skilled regulars and no longer dependent upon conscripts to fill their ranks. The Cold War had not abated, but Britain was now involved in fewer of the more localised military campaigns and emergencies of the kind that had, a few years earlier, required the deployment of large numbers of troops in such places as Korea, Cyprus, the Malayan peninsula, Kenya and the Suez Canal zone.

The government's decision to end National Service was made known to the British public in a curiously oblique fashion. In April 1957 Duncan Sandys, the Minister of Defence at the time, issued a White Paper which stated *inter alia* that the armed forces were to be reduced to half their current size, and were to become fully professional.[1] It followed from this that conscription would be coming to an end, but when? Young men approaching the age when they would, in the normal course of events, become liable for call-up needed to know whether or not they could instead go ahead with career, educational or matrimonial plans.

In the event there was some delay before the government deigned to announce the cutoff date of birth for registration for National Service. And frustrating though the delay clearly must have been to many, and typical of the heartlessness of bureaucracy, it could no doubt be justified by reasons of state. First of all, the military's operational requirements had to be considered, to ensure that the transition to a fully professional army, navy and air force proceeded as smoothly as possible, and without weakening the nation's defence capabilities. Then the impact upon allies and the reactions of potential enemies had also to be taken into account; at a time when tensions seemed to be heightening again in Europe, any sudden depletion of British army strength in Germany would have alarmed the Americans in particular, and might have encouraged aggressive moves by the Soviets or their East German allies.

Finally the date was agreed upon and made public, to audible sighs of relief or cries of anguish, depending upon one's date of birth: anyone born on or after 1 October 1939 would be spared call-up.

It was clear that the established pattern of training Chinese linguists and making use of their services, for however short a time, could not continue once the pool of university entrants and graduates and people of equivalent educational standard from which the linguists had been drawn dried up. For the time being courses under the aegis of the RAF continued to start at half-yearly intervals, the last one for servicemen (No. 11) running from September 1960 to August 1961. At the same time, the Air Ministry had begun to prepare for the eventual civilianisation of Chinese language training and work; it was understood that GCHQ would have to assume direct responsibility for this, and the role of the military, if any, would be a subordinate one.[2]

In 1970 RAF Tangmere closed after fifty years of often distinguished history, but some six years before this the Chinese language school, still nominally a part of JSSL, had already moved to North Luffenham in Rutland.[3] A casual observer dropping in on a Chinese class at Tangmere or North Luffenham during the 1960s would have come upon a scene not too different – at least superficially – from one which he might have witnessed at Wythall or Pucklechurch a decade earlier. Both Tangmere and North Luffenham remained as operational bases under RAF command, and the course instructors were still either serving officers, NCOs or Chinese civilians, at least one of the last-named group having been on the school's strength since the earliest days,[4] though whether the teaching methods had kept pace with the new approaches to language teaching emerging during the 1960s is a moot question which can not be answered here. The main visible difference, of course, would have been the fact that few if any of the students would be wearing service uniforms, for almost all were civilian employees of GCHQ.[5]

The changes that took place at the operational end in Hong Kong, as National Service came to an end, were much more profound. 367 Signals Unit was disbanded in 1962 and all remaining RAF elements of that unit were transferred from Little Sai Wan to Kai Tak;[6] GCHQ took over Little Sai Wan and its satellite operations, including Batty's, and the process of civilianisation was officially completed on 1 January 1964, when all SIGINT operations in Hong Kong passed formally under GCHQ control. Around this time and in the succeeding years, unsettling allegations were made by individuals both inside and outside the organisation, allegations of low morale and breaches of security and discipline. Few of these were ever properly substantiated, but their very existence must have been dispiriting to dedicated employees of GCHQ, and the situation during much of the 1960s may be contrasted with the less controversial and generally more harmonious atmosphere that had prevailed as long as the RAF remained in charge.[7]

There were changes, too, in the physical structure of operations in Hong Kong, as well as in the nature of those operations and even in their importance to the intelligence community. Batty's closed down in the mid-1960s, and its operational role was taken over by Tai Mo Shan, a station even closer to the clouds than Batty's – at the highest point on Hong Kong territory – which had already been in existence for several years as a Batty's outpost.[8] In 1982 GCHQ moved its entire operation from Little Sai Wan to Chung Hom Kok, a newly constructed facility on the south side of Hong Kong island.[9] While Tai Mo Shan may have been chosen at an earlier stage because it provided the clearest reception of Chinese ground to air signals (and vice versa), by the 1980s satellite communication was starting to assume greater importance as a source of SIGINT material, and this seems to be have been the main focus of operations at Chung Hom Kok.[10] But the move may also have been made simply because, in contrast to Little Sai Wan, Chung Hom Kok afforded those who were employed there, and now mainly lived off base in private quarters, an easier journey to and from work.

There are grounds for thinking that by this time the extent to which China should still be considered a serious military threat, justifying large-scale counter-intelligence efforts, was already being questioned. Some thirty years had elapsed since the ending of hostilities in Korea; the Cultural Revolution, too, had come and gone, and Deng Xiaoping's economic reforms were already in the wind. A 1985 publication claimed that by that year monitoring stations in Hong Kong had already started to direct their attention more towards Soviet naval movements in the western Pacific than to China itself.[11] Another sign that the USSR was once again regarded, as it had been in the immediate post-war period, as the primary military threat to the West – the 'evil empire' in Ronald Reagan's memorable phrase – was the conclusion of an agreement between the United States and China in 1979, shortly after the two governments had established diplomatic relations, to set up joint monitoring stations at Qitai and Korla in Xinjiang province, close to the Soviet frontier.[12]

The event that set in motion the final phase of the story which we have been unfolding was, of course, the Sino-British agreement to transfer sovereignty over Hong Kong to China on 1 July 1997. By the early 1990s Chung Hom Kok had switched over to remote control operation from Melbourne, with only a skeleton staff working on site,[13] and in January 1995 all the facilities there were dismantled and moved to the DSD (formerly DSB) base at Kojarena near Geraldton, Western Australia.[14] This is now said to be the main centre for monitoring Chinese radio communications, assisted by a post in Taiwan under United States control.[15] But one recent author on intelligence matters has claimed that even after July 1997 Britain continued to enjoy a limited monitoring capability in Hong Kong by means of listening devices implanted before the transfer of sovereignty in the walls of the former Prince of Wales barracks.[16] One assumes that once this claim appeared in print, the new occupants of the barracks, the People's Liberation Army, would have wasted no time in checking the situation out and, if necessary, having the offending devices removed.

The last official word on all these events is fittingly provided by that august British parliamentary publication, Hansard. In written answers to questions on 19 January 1998 it was reported that the sale of GCHQ's remaining properties in Hong Kong, consisting of twenty houses at Hong Lok Yuen which had accommodated officers, raised the princely sum of 12,451,316 pounds and 54 pence.[17]

But not quite the last word altogether. What of the bases in Britain where Chinese linguists were trained, and of those in Hong Kong where they worked some forty or fifty (or more) years ago? Wythall now houses a motor museum and a mobile home park, and the church which was a landmark at the entrance to the former base has been converted into executive offices. Part of Pucklechurch has been turned into a remand centre, and already by the 1960s, where Worth Matravers camp once stood, only ploughed fields were to be seen.[18] Tangmere alone retains some link with its RAF past, as the home of a military aviation museum. Fortunately, at or close to those stations where both Russian and Chinese linguists received their training, steps are now being taken to have commemorative plaques put in place to recall and honour their former functions.[19]

In Hong Kong, most of the original buildings at Batty's Belvedere and Tai Mo Shan reportedly remain *in situ*, though their present uses (if any) will naturally not be those of the years before the transfer of sovereignty. As for Little Sai Wan, given the land pressures in the territory and the immense value as real estate of its waterside location, it was perhaps inevitable that the former camp buildings would be torn down, to be replaced by towering residential blocks of the kind that now cover much of the Hong Kong's built-up area. Excellent bus services link the development directly to the MTR (Mass Transit Railway) system, whose extension right into the area now better known by its Cantonese name – Siu Sai Wan – is already in the planning stage.[20]

Yet against all the odds one relic of the past survives – the old camp access road which wound its way up the hillside on the east side of Little Sai Wan past the war cemetery to connect with the main Stanley road at Tai Tam Gap. It has taken on the air of a quiet country lane, used mainly by evening strollers and elderly ladies practicing their *taiji*.[21] No traffic passes along it now, save only the ghost of an occasional Bedford lorry in RAF blue straining its way up the hill before daybreak in low gear, ferrying linguists to their morning watch at Batty's.

Notes

1   Hickman (2004), p. 216. The news spread quickly through the linguists' ranks, and was noted by Mike Grindley (No. 3 Course) in his diary entry for 4 April 1958.

2   Memo from "M.4a" (unidentified) in Air Ministry files: AIR 2/11935 (RAF Personnel: Regular and National Service Entrants Selected for Training in Foreign Languages; Arrangements for Selection, Training and Conditions of Service, August 1955 to January 1961).

3   The move took place between 21 and 30 September 1964: AIR 28/1686 (Tangmere Operations Record Book, January 1961 to December 1965).

4   Jimmy Chuang (see Chapter 8), who taught on the first RAF Chinese course in 1955, is still clearly recognisable in a group photograph of JSSL instructors, taken at North Luffenham in 1969 and kindly made available by John Partridge.

5   In-service language training for GCHQ officers is to come to an end with the closure, announced in mid-2007, of the Foreign Office language school: Hencke (2007).

6   367/3.41.

7   Ball (1996), pp. 481-483; Campbell/Kane (1980), pp. 738-744 and 774-776; Richelson/Ball (1986), p. 23; West (1988), p. 302. Jock Kane, a former GCHQ officer in Hong Kong, wrote a book setting out his allegations of misconduct at Little Sai Wan; a High Court injunction preventing its publication remains in force to this day: Hansard, Written Answers to Questions, 25 February 1993; West (1988), p. 293. A few cases of Chinese civilian employees passing classified information to the authorities in the Chinese mainland had come to light even before the transfer of responsibility to GCHQ: Ball (1986), pp. 481-482.

8   Mike Wallace (No. 7 Course) remembers being sent to Tai Mo Shan on rotation in 1959-60, and it was reportedly the scene of unusually frantic monitoring activity on 1 May 1960. That was the night on which the U-2 spy plane piloted by Gary Powers was shot down over the Soviet Union, an event that effectively undermined the summit meeting between President Eisenhower and Premier Khrushchev due to take place shortly thereafter.

9   Ball (1996), p. 483; Richelson/Ball (1985), p. 23.

10   Minnick (2003).

11   Richelson/Ball (1985), p. 206.

12   Richelson/Ball (1985), pp. 171-172. West (1988), pp. 289-290, states on dubious authority that the United States received permission to establish these monitoring stations 'after Nixon's visit to China,' which took place in 1972.

13   Bamford (2001), p. 541.

14   Ball (1996), p. 49; *en.wikipedia.org/wiki/Defence_Signals_ Directorate.*

15   Minnick (2003).

16   Bamford (2001), p. 542.

17   Hansard, Written Answers to Questions, 19 January 1998, answer given by the late Derek Fatchett, then Under-Secretary of State for Foreign and Commonwealth Affairs.

18   Information from John Norrish.

19   At Tangmere in 2003 and Pucklechurch in 2006, initiatives taken by the Royal Air Force Linguists' Association (RAFLING), which is also planning a plaque ceremony at Wythall too.

20   *en.wikipedia.org/wiki/Siu_Sai_Wan.*

21   *T'ai chi* in the old Wade-Giles romanisation, and for those former RAF linguists who still remember their G.R.: *tayjyi.*

BIBLIOGRAPHY

Primary sources (archived documents and personal reminiscences)

The National Archives at Kew in southwest London, formerly known as the Public Record Office, are the depository for official records that have been declassified and are now available for public inspection. All of the files listed below were consulted by one or other of the authors, and in footnotes they are usually cited by their serial numbers alone; however the full title of the file is given when it is referred to for the first time in a chapter.

AIR 2/11394 (October 1952 to August 1955) and *AIR 2/11395* (August 1955 to January 1961). RAF Personnel: Regular and National Service Entrants Selected for Training in Foreign Languages; Arrangements for Selection, Training and Conditions of Service.
AIR 2/12599. Language Training, 1956-1960.
AIR 2/13255. RAF Personnel: Language Training Requirements, Minutes.
AIR 2/16320. North Luffenham: Organisation, 1962-1972.
DEFE 10/343. Services Language Training Committee: Minutes of Meetings and Memoranda, 1956-1958 and Services Language Policy Committee: Minutes of Meetings and Memoranda, 1958-1962.

The following files are Operations Record Books kept by the various RAF stations and units at which Chinese linguists were trained or subsequently worked:
AIR 28/1291. Wythall, May 1951 to December 1955.
AIR 28/1331. Little Sai Wan, July 1956 to December 1959.
AIR 28/1410. Pucklechurch, January 1956 to December 1959.
AIR 28/1426. Tangmere, January 1956 to December 1960.
AIR 28/1448. Wythall, January 1956 to December 1959.
AIR 28/1628 and *AIR 28/1629.* North Luffenham, January 1961 to December 1966.

AIR 28/1686. Tangmere, January 1961 to December 1965.
AIR 29/2284. No. 367 SU, August 1954 to December 1955.
AIR 29/3034. Worth Matravers (No. 407 SU), December 1955 to August 1963.
AIR 29/3764. No. 367 SU, Little Sai Wan, 1956-1963.

* * * * * *

367 Association. A private collection of personal reminiscences by former members of 367 Signals Unit (Little Sai Wan, Hong Kong). Ongoing series (12 books published to date). [Cited as: 367/book no., page no.]

The authors have gratefully relied, to a significant extent, on the oral and written reminiscences of many who served as Chinese linguists. Their contributions are individually acknowledged in the Preface, as well as in the text and footnotes.

Secondary sources (books and periodical articles)

Aldrich (1998). Aldrich, Richard. Espionage, Security and Intelligence in Britain, 1945-70. Manchester: Manchester University Press, 1998.

Aldrich (2001). Aldrich, Richard J. The Hidden Hand: Britain, America and Cold War Secret Intelligence. London: John Murray, 2001.

Ball (1996). Ball, Desmond, "Over and Out: Signals Intelligence (SIGINT) in Hong Kong," Intelligence and National Security 11.3 (July 1996), pp. 474-496.

Baller (1900). Baller, F. W. An Analytical Chinese-English Dictionary. Shanghai: China Inland Mission and American Presbyterian Mission Press, 1900.

Bamford (1982). Bamford, James. The Puzzle Palace: A Report on America's Most Secret Agency. Boston: Houghton Mifflin Co., 1982.

Bamford (2001). Bamford, James. Body of Secrets. New York: Doubleday, 2001.

Bennett/Bennett (2003). Bennett, Richard M. and Bennett, Katie. The Mechanics of an Oppressive State: UK Intelligence and Security Report, August 2003. Online at *www.informationclearinghouse.info/article4463.htm* and *www.informationclearinghouse.info/article4464.htm*.

Bright (2003). Bright, Martin, "From barracks to fun park." The Observer 31 August 2003.

Campbell (2000). Campbell, Duncan, "Inside Echelon," published online in Telepolis (Hannover), 25 July 2000, at *www.heise.de/ tp/r4/artikel/6/6929/1.html, cyberdelix.net/parvati/6929.html* and *farshores.250free.com/s_ech03.htm*.

Campbell/Kane (1980). Campbell, Duncan and Kane, Jock, "The spies who spend what they like" and "Jock Kane's story," New Statesman 16 May 1980, pp. 738-744 and 23 May 1980, pp. 774-777.

Davies (2004). Davies, Philip H.J. MI6 and the Machinery of Spying. London and Portland, Oregon: Frank Cass Publishers, 2004.

Dorril (2000). Dorril, Stephen. MI6: Fifty Years of Special Operations. London: Fourth Estate, 2000.

Elliott/Shukman (2003). Elliott, Geoffrey and Shukman, Harold. Secret Classrooms: A Memoir of the Cold War. London: St. Ermin's Press, 2002 (hardcover)/2003 (paperback). [Text references are to the paperback edition.]

Halsey (1988). Halsey, A.H. (ed.). British Social Trends Since 1900: A Guide to the Changing Social Structure of Britain. 2nd edition, Basingstoke : Macmillan, 1988.

Hayter Report (1961). University Grants Committee. Report of the Sub-Committee on Oriental, Slavonic, East European and African Studies. London: Her Majesty's Stationery Office, 1961. [Generally referred to as the "Hayter Report" after the Sub-Committee's Chairman, Sir William Hayter.]

Hencke (2007). Hencke, David. "Government axes Foreign Office language school." Guardian Unlimited, 3 July 2007.

Hickman (2004). Hickman, Tom. The Call-Up: A History of National Service. London: Headline Book Publishing, 2004.

Hinsley/Stripp (1993). Hinsley, F.H. and Stripp, Alan (editors). Code Breakers: The Inside Story of Bletchley Park. Oxford: Oxford University Press, 1993.

Hockett/Fang (1944). Hockett, Charles F. and Fang, Chaoying. Spoken Chinese (Volume I). Washington DC: 'Published for the United States Armed Forces Institute by the Linguistic Society of America and the Intensive Language Program American Council of Learned Societies'.. [U.S. War Department Education Manual: EM506.]

Hockett/Fang (1945). Hockett, Charles F. and Fang, Chaoying. Spoken Chinese (Volume II). Washington DC: 'Published for the United States Armed Forces Institute by the Linguistic Society of America and the Intensive Language Program American Council of Learned Societies'. [U.S. War Department Education Manual: EM507.]

Hutchinson (2006). Hutchinson, Robert. Elizabeth's Spy Master. London: Weidenfeld & Nicolson, 2006.

168

Keegan (2003). Keegan, John. <u>Intelligence in War: Knowledge of the Enemy from Napoleon to Al-Qaeda</u>. Toronto: Key Porter Books Limited, 2003.

Lee (1999). Lee, Michael, "The Joint Services School for Linguists," <u>The Linguist</u> 38.4 (1999), pp. 118-119.

Macksey (2003). Macksey, Kenneth. <u>The Searchers: Radio Intercepts in Two World Wars</u>. London: Cassell, 2003.

Mathews (1931). Mathews, R. H. <u>Mathews' Chinese-English dictionary</u>. Shanghai: China Inland Mission and Presbyterian Mission Press, 1931. [*Mathews (1943)* = Revised American edition, Cambridge, Mass.: Harvard University Press, 1943.]

Minnick (2003). Minnick, Wendell, "Spook Mountain: How US spies on China," <u>Asia Times</u>, 6 March 2003, also online at *www.atimes. com/atimes/China/EC06Ad03.html.*

Mirsky (1980). Mirsky, Jonathan, "Film on spy base will start a storm," <u>The Observer</u>, 8 June 1980, p. 10.

Phillips (1948). Phillips, Clifford H. P. <u>Handbook of Royal Air Force Terminology: English-Chinese</u>. London: Air Ministry, 1948,

Ramparts Magazine (1972). "U.S. Electronic Espionage: A Memoir," <u>Ramparts</u> 11.2 (August 1972), pp. 35-50. [Transcript of interview with a former National Security Agency officer.]

Richelson/Ball (1985). Richelson, Jeffrey T. and Ball, Desmond. <u>The Ties That Bind: Intelligence Cooperation between the UKUSA Countries – the United Kingdom, the United States of America, Canada, Australia and New Zealand</u>. North Sydney: Allen and Unwin Australia Pty Ltd, 1985.

Russell (1969). Russell, Bertrand. The Autobiography of Bertrand Russell: The Middle Years, 1914-1944. Boston: Little, Brown and Company, 1969. [Bantam Books edition.]

Sawatsky (1982). Sawatsky, John. For Services Rendered: Leslie James Bennett and the RCMP Security Service. Toronto: Doubleday Canada Limited, 1982.

Simon (1942-44). Simon, Walter. Chinese Sentence Series. 3 volumes, London: A. Probsthain, 1942-44.

Simon (1944a). Simon, Walter. How to Study and Write Chinese Characters: Chinese Radicals and Phonetics, with an Analysis of the 1200 Chinese Basic Characters. London: Lund, Humphries and Co. Ltd., 1944.

Simon (1944b). Simon, Walter. 1200 Chinese Basic Characters, An Elementary Text Book Adapted From the 'Thousand Character Lessons'. London: Lund, Humphries and Co. Ltd., [1944].

Simon (1947). Simon, Walter. A Beginner's Chinese-English Dictionary of the National Language (Gwoyeu). London: Lund, Humphries and Co. Ltd., 1947. [2nd revised edition 1958.]

Simon/Chao (1945). Simon, Walter and Chao, T.C. Structure Drill In Chinese. London: Lund, Humphries and Co. Ltd., 1945.

Simon/Lu (1954). Simon, Walter and Lu, C.H. Chinese National Language (Gwoyeu) Reader and Guide to Conversation. London: Lund Humphries and Co. Ltd., [1954].

Smith (1998). Smith, Michael. Station X: Decoding Nazi Secrets. New York: TV Books, 1998.

Smith (2000). Smith, Michael. The Emperor's Codes: The Role of Bletchley Park in Breaking Japan's Secret Ciphers. New York: Bantam Books, 2000.

Summers (1990). Summers, Harry J., Jr. <u>Korean War Almanac</u>. New York: Facts on File, Inc., 1990.

Thomas (1988). Thomas, Andy, "British Signals Intelligence after the Second World War," <u>Intelligence and National Security</u> 3.4 (October 1988), pp. 103-110.

Twitchett/Fairbank (1978). Twitchett, Denis C. and Fairbank, John K. (edd.). <u>The Cambridge History of China</u>. 13 volumes, Cambridge and New York: Cambridge University Press, 1978-2003. Volume 10 (Late Ch'ing, 1800 to 1911), Part I, published in 1978.

West (1986). West, Nigel. <u>GCHQ: The Wireless War</u>. London: Weidenfeld & Nicolson, 1986.

West (1988). West, Nigel. <u>The Sigint Secrets: The Signals Intelligence War, 1900 to Today, Including the Persecution of Gordon Welchman</u>. New York: William Morrow and Company. Inc., 1988.

Woodhead (2005). Woodhead, Leslie. <u>My Life as a Spy</u>. London: Macmillan, 2005.

Wright (1987). Wright, Peter. <u>Spycatcher: The Candid Autobiography of a Senior Intelligence Officer</u>. Toronto: Stoddart Publishing Co. Limited, 1987.

APPENDIX A

TABLE OF RAF CHINESE COURSES, 1955-1961

No. 1 Course (October 1955 to September 1956)

Location: RAF Wythall (8 miles south of Birmingham)
Programme director: Sqn Ldr John D. Wright
Course directors: Sqn Ldr Wright (to June 1956), Flt Lt B.S.J.
"Bennie" Piff (June to September 1956)
Number of students: 39 at start of course (all RAF National
Servicemen)
15 left course to study at the School of Oriental and African
Studies, London (SOAS) as officer cadets, 2 subsequently
returned to Wythall
1 student left before final exam, 25 completed course, 24 were
posted to Hong Kong and 1 remained in UK as instructor
Sources: National Archives (file AIR 28/1448) and personal
knowledge of the authors

No. 2 Course (April 1956 to April 1957)

Locations: RAF Wythall (April to June 1956 and September 1956
to April 1957); RAF Worth Matravers, Dorset (July to September
1956)
Programme director: Sqn Ldr Wright
Course director: Sqn Ldr Wright
Number of students: 29 (25 RAF, 3 Army NCOs and 1 Army
Private)
Source: National Archives (file AIR 28/1448)

No. 3 Course (October 1956 to October 1957)

Locations: RAF Worth Matravers (October 1956 to April 1957;
RAF Pucklechurch, 8 miles northeast of Bristol (April to October
1957)
Programme director: Sqn Ldr Wright

Course director: Sqn Ldr Wright
Number of students: 39 at start of course (all RAF National Servicemen, 1 subsequently became regular)
3 left course to study at SOAS as officer cadets
5 left in mid-course for other reasons
31 completed course
Sources: National Archives (file AIR 28/1448) and course informants

No. 4 Course (May 1957 to April 1958)

Location: RAF Pucklechurch
Programme director: Sqn Ldr Wright
Course director: Sqn Ldr Wright
Number of students: 22 at start of course (21 RAF National Servicemen, 1 RAF regular)
1 left in mid-course
21 completed course
Source: Course informant

No. 5 Course (October 1957 to October 1958)

Location: RAF Pucklechurch
Programme directors: Sqn Ldr Wright (October 1957 to September 1958); Flt Lt J.A. "Joe" Cant (September to October 1958)
Course directors: Flt Lt M.H.C. Burns (October 1957 to January 1958); Flt Lt P.J.W. "Paddy" Raine (January to October 1958)
Number of students: 38 at start of course (all RAF National Servicemen)
3 left course to study at SOAS as officer cadets, 1 other subsequently withdrew
34 completed course
Sources: Course informants

No. 6 Course (April 1958 to April 1959)

Location: RAF Pucklechurch
Programme directors: Sqn Ldr Wright (April to September 1958); Flt Lt Cant (September 1958 to January 1959); Sqn Ldr W.D. "Dickie" Blythe (January to April 1959)
Course director: Flt Lt Peter George
Number of students: 42 (41 RAF National Servicemen, a few subsequently becoming regulars; 1 Army NCO)
1 left in mid-course
41 completed course (3 posted to GCHQ Cheltenham, rest to Hong Kong)
Sources: National Archives (file AIR 28/1410) and course informants

No. 7 Course (October 1958 to October 1959)

Location: RAF Pucklechurch
Programme director: Sqn Ldr Blythe
Course director: Flt Lt Raine
Number of students: 44 at start of course (all RAF National Servicemen)
40 successfully completed course, 4 assigned to other trades
39 posted to Hong Kong, 1 remained in UK as instructor
Sources: Course informants

No. 8 Course (April 1959 to April 1960)

Locations: RAF Pucklechurch (April to September 1959); RAF Tangmere, Sussex (September 1959 to April 1960)
Programme director: Sqn Ldr Blythe
Course director:
Number of students: 28 at start of course (16 RAF National Servicemen, 3 RAF regulars, 1 Army NCO, 8 Army Privates)
1 left in mid-course
27 completed course
Sources: National Archives (file AIR 28/1410) and course informant

No. 9 Course (October 1959 to October 1960)

Location: RAF Tangmere
Programme director: Sqn Ldr Blythe
Course director:
Number of students: 12-14 at start of course (3 RAF regulars, rest RAF National Servicemen)
1 failed to complete course
Source: Course informant

No. 10 Course (April 1960 to April 1961)

Location: RAF Tangmere
Programme director: Flt Lt Clifford H.P. Phillips
Course director:
Number of students: 12 (mainly RAF, some Army)
Sources: Informants from other courses

No. 11 Course (September 1960 to August 1961)

Location: RAF Tangmere
Programme director: Flt Lt Phillips
Course director: F/O Peter Cousins
Number of students: 15 (12 RAF National Servicemen, 1 RAF regular, 2 Army regulars)
Sources: Course informants

Note: The authors are well aware that the above information is incomplete and in some cases of doubtful accuracy. They would appreciate receiving (by email to *RAFChinese@gmail.com*) any corrections and any further details that readers may be able to supply.

APPENDIX B

WHY 'BATTY'S BELVEDERE'?

Kenneth Wilson

Substantial research has been undertaken by several interested parties to determine why the RAF installation on Victoria Peak was referred to as Batty's Belvedere.

General guide books refer to a Governor constructing a summer residence with formal gardens on the summit of Victoria Peak, possibly Sir Richard MacDonnell whose tenure was 1865-72, since his dates coincide with such references. Contemporary photographs show the gardens to the property ran down from a site which must have been on or near the RAF installation, and which appears to have been named 'The Eyrie'.

It is clear from these photographs, however, that a structure, which from its shape must be a belvedere, existed on a mound some little distance to the west of The Eyrie. Research suggests that this belvedere was constructed by a naval captain by the name of Batty, and the belvedere appears to have been open to the public as a viewpoint.

From Britain's earliest occupation of Hong Kong, the Royal Navy maintained a signal station on the Peak, and this station appears to have been taken over by the RAF after World War II, with the Navy concentrating their operations on Stonecutter's Island. The mound upon which the belvedere stood can be clearly identified still, although, today, it bears what is probably a communications station.

It is not known what name the Navy attached to their signal station, but it seems a reasonable supposition that, with the close proximity of the belvedere constructed by a Navy man, the signal station became known as Batty's Belvedere, a name which the RAF inherited.

No, 1 Chinese Course   Paper 3

End of Term Examination - March 1956

Chinese (G.R.) to English

Time allowed: 1 hour   Total marks: 100

1.   SHIANN TZAY DE PEN SHEH JI FEI DE BII JIAW YII CHYAN DE FEI JI KUAY DE

DUO LE, ERL CHIEE NENG GOW FEI DE HEEN GAU.   GANG JIANQ JUOH DE SHYR HOW, JIAH

SHYY YUAN YAW TEH BYE JUH YIH TA DE SUH DUH GEN HARNG SHIANN (LUH).

(Marks: 15)

2.   DIANN DENG JIANQ YIH SHIOU LII DIANN SHIANN YII HOW WOO MEN JIOW TING DAW

LE FEI JI HU JIOW DE SHINN HAW.   TA SHUO TA DE FA DONQ JI YEOU MAU BINQ.

(Marks: 14)

3.   DIH ELL TSYH DAH JANN DAA CHII JANQ CHAH BUH DUO LEANG NIAN YII HOW, MEEI

GWO JIOW BANG JUH ING GWO GEN CHYI TA DE GWO JIA BAA DER GWO DAA BAY LE.

(Marks: 14)

4.   TZAY WOO DE NAN HAIRTZ MEI LI FARNG TZ YAW DAW SHYUE SHIAW CHIUH YII CHYAN,

TA SHUO TA DE TOUR , YA, TOEI, GE BEY, LIAN TADE SHOOU.JYR TOU DOU TERNG LE.

WOO GAW SUH TA, SHERME REN YEOU NAH ME KUU YI DINQ KUAY YAW SYY LE, TZUEY

HAO YEANG JEH ME KUU DE BINQ SH TZAY YI GEH SHYUE SHIAW LII.

(Marks: 14)

5.   IN WEY WOO SHING CHYI WUU, SHYR ELL DEAN JONG, YAW HWEI JIA CHIUH, WOO

JYR BAN DE SHYR JIAN KEE YII GAE BIANN LE MA.   RU GUOO BUH GAE TUOO LE,   WOO

JIOW BUH NENG CHIUH.   (Marks: 14)

6.   WOO DE TORNG SHYUE JIA LII YEOU GEH SHEAU HUA YUAN, HUA YUAN HOW MIANN YEOU

YI KUAY KONG DIH.   TA TZAY NAH LII TZAW LE YI GEH WOANG CHYOU CHAANG.   WOO

CHARNG CHARNG DAW NAH LII CHIUH DAA LE.

(Marks: 14)

7.   NII SHUO DER DUEY.   KEE SH, NII WEY SHER ME TIH JIOW JYH-DUH SHUO HUAH.

NII JY DAW, YAW SH WOOMEN ANN J JEH JIOW SHYH DE JYH DUH TARN TARN LE, JIOW

NII BUH NENG JEH YANQ SHU FWU DE SWEI BIANN DE, GEN WOO SHUO HUAH LE.

(Marks: 15)

APPENDIX D

Time Allowed: 1½ hours   Total marks: 100

Part 1 (50 marks)   ANSWER ANY 5 OUT OF 6 QUESTIONS

1.   He told me that he was a wireless operator in the Royal Air Force, also
that he had to make contact with his radio control station before his aircraft
was permitted to take off.   (10 marks)

2.   The Far Eastern Fleet consisted of an aircraft carrier, a battleship, two
cruisers, nine destroyers and several gun boats.   (10 marks)

3.   Although tanks of the 50th division encountered heavy enemy field gun and
anti tank gun fire their casualties were not heavy.   (10 marks)

4.   At present there is no air passenger service from Hong Kong to the Chinese
mainland, but one can go by train from the JEOU LONG peninsular or by ship to
any of the south eastern ports.   (10 marks)

5.   I received a letter yesterday from a friend who lives in the country,
inviting me to come and stay with him for a few days, but as I am so busy I
won't be able to go.   (10 marks)

6.   When the railway porter saw how much luggage I had, he immediately ran to
the booking office and brought one of the luggage trolleys.
                                                         (10 marks)

Part 2 (50 marks)

        Write an essay on one of the following:

        1.   "The Chinese Language".

        2.   A journey by sea from England to Hong Kong.

        3.   An aircraft accident over enemy territory which required you as one
        of the crew to descend by parachute and your subsequent journey back to
        your base.

NOTE: Students should note that half of the total marks are allotted to this essay.

End of Term Test – June 1956
English to Chinese (Geoff Russell)

178

APPENDIX E

End of Term Examination – June 1956

Chinese Characters

Time allowed: 30 minutes   Marks: 50

(A)   Translate the following sentences into Chinese: ANY TWO FROM PART A:-

1.   They **continued** to maintain contact with the ground station.   (10)

2.   I can see the control tower clearly on the right hand side.   (10)

3.   We must inspect our weapons before taking off.   (10)

(B)   Write the characters for the following phrases:

(1) to ascend   (6) useless

(2) to descend   (7) faulty

(3) to surrender   (8) throttle

(4) to apply brakes   (9) altitude

(5) south wind   (10) towards the east
                                                                   (10)

(C)   Translate the following sentences into English:

我們總得把他們投降的事情報告總司令

那是一個有放射能的區域我們不可進去得從外邊走.

總會指定了一個代表來檢察我們的工作我們要小心

這是很有用的儀器請不要毀壞了.

檢察長總要告發他所做的不對的事情.

End of Term Test – June 1956
Chinese Characters (Geoff Russell)

179

APPENDIX F

J/T EXAMINATION.

ENGLISH/CHINESE.

TIME ALLOWED ... I HOUR.

MARKS .... 100.

I. THE MOST DANGEROUS CONDITIONS FOR PRODUCING ICE ACCRETION ON AN AIRCRAFT ARE TEMPERATURES OF O DEGREES TO MINUS IO DEGREES WHEN FLYING IN CUMULUS CLOUD.

2. APART FROM THE PILOT AND SECOND PILOT, THE BOMBER AIRCRAFT HAD A WIRELESS-OPERATOR AND GUNNER.

3. WE MUST BE VERY ATTENTIVE WHEN STUDYING THIS SUBJECT, SO THAT WE CAN USE IT CORRECTLY IN THE FUTURE.

4. IF TIME PERMITS, WE SHOULD BE ABLE TO STAY AT THE HOTEL FOR A MEAL.

5. ALTHOUGH THE DANCE-HALL IS ALWAYS CROWDED ON A SATURDAY NIGHT, I LIKE TO GO THERE AND DANCE WITH MY GIRL-FRIEND.

J/T Final Examination – September 1956
English/Chinese (Geoff Russell)

Opposite page:
map of Hong Kong Central and part of Kowloon – 1950s
(John Henty)

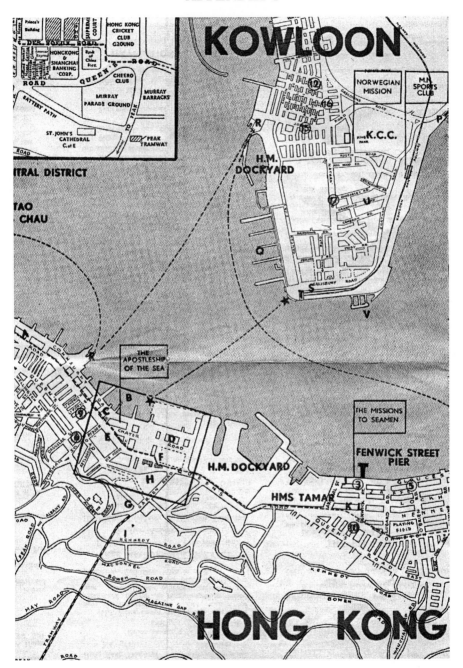

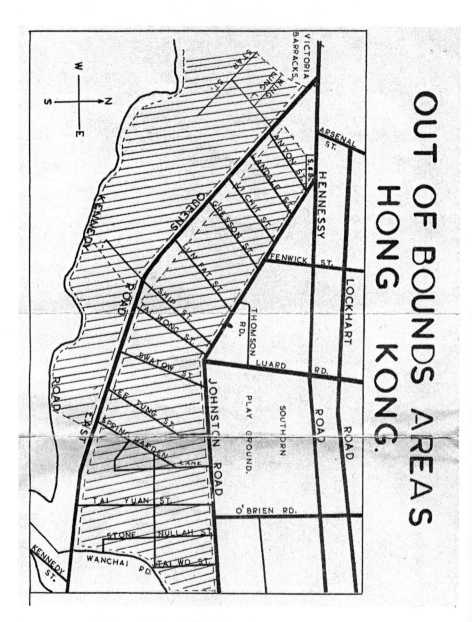

Out of Bounds Areas – Hong Kong – 1950s
(John Henty)

APPENDIX I

1

R.A.F. Form 64

ROYAL AIR FORCE

AIRMAN'S SERVICE BOOK

Instructions to Airman.

1. You will be held personally responsible for the safe custody of this book.

2. You will always carry the book on your person both at home and abroad.

3. You must produce the book whenever called upon to do so by a competent authority, civil, naval, military or air.

4. You must not alter or make any entry in the book, and disobedience of this order will be treated as a serious offence.

5. Should you consider that any entry in the book is lacking or incorrect, or should you lose the book, you will report the matter to your immediate superior in Royal Air Force. Any change in name or address of person to be informed of casualties must be reported immediately to your Commanding Officer.

6. If you have not already done so, you are strongly advised to make a Will by following the instructions given on pages 8 and 9 of this book. Even if your possessions are small it will simplify matters for all concerned if you make a Will showing how you wish them to be disposed of in the event of your death. Insertion of the name of the " Person to be informed of casualties " on page 2 is NOT a Will and has no bearing on the disposition of your property. Should you wish to alter your Will at a later date, you can always make out another by following the same instructions.

Extract from Airmen's Service Book – RAF Form 64
(Bernard Morton)

APPENDIX J

FOR YOUR INFORMATION.

You are now in the Independent State of Libya. Tripoli, 20 miles away, is the capital of the Western Province which is a good modern city with excellent shops etc.

TRANSPORT.

Taxis are available but are very expensive. Lifts can be given to town but no guarantee can be given of a return lift to Idris.

SWIMMING.

There are two pools on the Station and an Army Beach open to Airmen in Tripoli. Officers are Honorary Members of the Tripoli Beach Club.

CINEMA.

Four programmes weekly - Monday, Wednesday, Friday and Sunday on camp. See bills in reception. Seats are bookable at the Guardroom.

Transients are not to leave the camp area without prior permission to do so.

We hope you have had a pleasant stay at R.A.F. Idris. If you have any suggestions for improvements please let us know.

W.G. P.G.D. FARR o.b.e., d.f.c.

YOUR SUGGESTIONS PLEASE

No. .... *Rank* .... *Name* ....

Destination ....

184

TRANSIT HOTEL
ROYAL AIR FORCE, IDRIS

You are accommodated in

Block............................... Room...................................

MEAL TIMES.

    Breakfast   07.30 - 09.00
    Lunch   12.30 - 13.30
    Dinner   18.30 - 20.00

BAR HOURS.

    Officers   12.00 - 13.30   18.00 - 23.00
    S.N.C.O.s   12.00 - 13.30   18.00 - 23.00
    Other Ranks   12.00 - 13.30   18.00 - 22.00

DRESS REGULATIONS.

Normal rules apply - shorts will not be worn after 19.00 hours.

CURRENCY.

Sterling and Local Currency is accepted in Transit only. If sightseeing in Tripoli Local Currency must be used.

SOUVENIRS.

Souvenirs of your stay are on sale in the Reception Office and Bars. It would be appreciated if Ash Trays, Cups, Thermos Flasks and other items provided for your benefit are not removed for this purpose.

No 1 Chinese Course after one year's language training
(Bernard Morton)

Locker in Hut No 8 at RAF Wythall
(Bernard Morton)

Top: Flight Lieutenant J. Cant (Peter Bernasconi)
Bottom: Squadron Leader J.D. Wright (Peter Bernasconi)

Postcard view of Hong Kong Harbour ~ October 1956
(Reg Hunt)

Postcard view of Hong Kong Harbour ~ October 2006
(John Henty)